The Anasazi

The Anasazi

ELEANOR H. AYER

WALKER AND COMPANY
NEW YORK

First published in the United States of America in 1993
by Walker Publishing Company, Inc.

Published simultaneously in Canada by Thomas Allen & Son
Canada, Limited, Markham, Ontario

Library of Congress Cataloging-in-Publication Data
Ayer, Eleanor H.
The Anasazi / Eleanor H. Ayer.
p. cm.
Includes bibliographical references and index.
Summary: Examines what is known about the Anasazi civilization,
from the arrival of the Ancient Ones in North America 14,000 years
ago to the lives of their present-day descendants, the Pueblo.
ISBN 0-8027-8184-5 (C).—ISBN 0-8027-8185-3 (R)
1. Pueblo Indians—Juvenile literature.   2. Pueblo Indians—
Antiquities—Juvenile literature.   [1. Pueblo Indians.   2. Indians
of North America—Southwest, New.]   I. Title.
E99.P9A94   1993
979'.01—dc20   92-14701
CIP
AC

Printed in the United States of America

2   4   6   8   10   9   7   5   3   1

For my mother, Shirley T. Hubbard,
whose fascination with history and archaeology
most certainly led to my own.

CONTENTS

Acknowledgments

Grateful thanks are extended to the archaeologists and interpretive specialists at the national parklands mentioned in this book. Their help in acquiring photographs and in verifying information is much appreciated, particularly in light of the smaller staffs and increased workload that face our national parks today.

Special thanks are extended to the following people who took time to read all or parts of the manuscript for accuracy: Ms. Linda Martin, Mesa Verde National Park; Mr. John Andresen, Casa Grande Ruins National Monument; Mr. David Breternitz, Professor Emeritus of Anthropology, University of Colorado, and current Director of the Mesa Verde Regional Research Center at Dove Creek, Colorado.

The Ancient Ones

About 14,000 years ago, a land bridge—at some points as wide as a thousand miles—connected the continents of Asia and North America at the Bering Strait. Across this land bridge and southward down the continent of North America, ancient people wandered from Asia into a new land. Many generations later, some of their descendants settled in the Four Corners region of what is now the United States—where Utah, Colorado, Arizona, and New Mexico join.

Archaic people, as we call these early nomads of the arid Southwest, roamed the land hunting and gathering food. The men hunted mammoths, bison, and smaller animals. The women and children gathered nuts and berries. Because they were nomads, the Archaic people made their homes in caves and simple lean-tos instead of building houses. These caves or alcoves were not dark passageways deep in the sides of mountains but shallow recesses at the base of high

ANASAZI COUNTRY

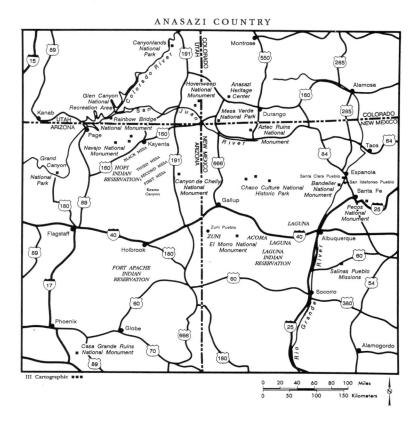

sandstone cliffs. Such homes were well suited to receive light from the sun or a bright full moon.

As they wandered, the Archaic people found a need for containers to hold the food they were gathering. From the long, tough spines of the yucca plants that grew all around, they began weaving baskets. So important was basket making that it brought a whole new way of life to the Archaic people. The period that followed, beginning about A.D. 1, is known as the Basket Maker era.

Basket Makers were the first in a group of ancient Southwest Indians called Anasazi, a Navajo word meaning "ancient ones." The Anasazi were a short and stocky people. Many had thick, black, straight hair and medium- to dark-brown skin, like some modern native Americans. They spoke a language like that of some modern Pueblo people.

Because they lived at a time before their history was recorded, the Anasazi are said to be prehistoric peo-

Anasazi handprint in sandstone was found near present-day Canyonlands National Park in Utah. The "artist" placed his hand on the rock and, using paint made of animal fat and vegetable dyes—like that for pictographs—blew the paint through a tube cut from a hollowed-out reed. This made a reverse or negative handprint in the stone. (*Courtesy of Greg Gnesios*)

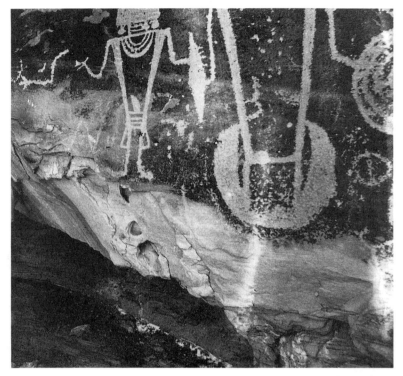

These petroglyphs at Dinosaur National Monument, on the Colorado–Utah border, were made by the Fremont people, who lived before and during the Early Basket Maker period. *(Courtesy of National Park Service)*

ple. Although they left no written language, they did leave, on large stones and on alcove walls, thousands of petroglyphs (pictures carved or etched into stone) and pictographs (paintings made on stone).

CLUES TO THE PAST

The petroglyphs and pictographs give us a few hints about life in Early Basket Maker times. To learn more, scientists study artifacts, including baskets, bones, and bits of clothing, found in Anasazi homes and villages. By studying these artifacts, they are able to piece together a picture of life in Early Basker Maker times.

How do archaeologists unearth these artifacts from ancient sites? When they find a spot they wish to excavate, they first divide it into sections and make a grid on paper. Each section is given its own code so that a record can be made of the exact location of each artifact. Different methods of digging are used, depending on what is being excavated.

Most digging is done with picks, trowels, and hoes. Heavy earth-moving equipment must be used very carefully, for fear of damaging delicate artifacts. As layers of soil are unearthed, workers clear dirt from the items they uncover. They take this dirt to wooden racks set up at the site and sift it through fine mesh screens, which collect tiny objects such as shells or pieces of bone.

Once the artifacts at a site have been discovered, the archaeologist tries to determine their ages. There are several ways of telling, or at least coming close. One is called dendrochronology, the science of tree ring dating. This method is used for telling the age of a piece of wood. Every year a tree is alive, it adds a new growth ring. You can see these rings in the log or stump when the tree is cut. Some of the rings will be

An archaeological excavation at Mesa Verde National Park, Colorado. *(Courtesy of Mesa Verde National Park)*

wide and some will be narrow, depending on how wet or dry the year was. But the ring pattern is the same for trees growing in the same area. By studying the growth rings of poles cut for early houses, archaeologists can tell the approximate age of an Anasazi site.

Another method is ceramic dating, which archaeologists use when studying pottery or other clay objects. They look at the color and design of pieces and study the materials, tools, and techniques used to make them. This information gives clues to the age of the pieces. By gathering and studying many pieces, archaeologists can come very close to telling the age of a site.

Studying metal particles in pieces of burned clay is another way of telling the age of artifacts. Scientists know that at the north and south poles, the earth's magnetic pull is straight down. But the location of the poles has changed over the years. Today they are not in exactly the same place that they were 2,000 years ago. To tell the age of a site, archaeologists determine the direction that the magnetic particles in a piece of ancient clay are pointing. By knowing when the pole was located here and comparing it with the location of the poles today, archaeologists can determine the age of the piece of clay.

But there is a limit to what archaeology can tell us about people. Charles Avery Amsden, who spent many years studying the Anasazi, explains that "Archaeology tells much of the life of the body and the work of the hands, but little of the life of the spirit and the work of the mind. Like a painting, it can give us no more than the eye can see." Our imaginations must take over from there.

STAYING ALIVE IN PLATEAU COUNTRY

The Anasazi lived on a high, flat tableland known as the Colorado Plateau. Because the American Southwest is so dry, finding water was very important.

Many Early Basket Makers traveled at first toward the northern and eastern sections of the plateau, along the San Juan River. They looked for streams and springs, and for the mesa tops that received the most rain and snow.

Like the Archaic people, most Early Basket Makers roamed the land rather than settling in one place. A shallow alcove made a good home for a few nights until it was time to move on again, in search of new animals and wild fruits and nuts. These alcoves were tucked into the sides of mesas, the large flat-topped mountains common in the Southwest.

Most of the Anasazi's days were spent just trying to stay alive—finding water and shelter and wandering in search of game. The Early Basket Makers had no guns or bows and arrows, so to hunt rabbits and other small animals, they used netlike snares woven from yucca and human hair. The snares were often four feet across, and the men would string them for nearly 200 feet along a good hunting area. One hunter might place the net across a dry creek or other likely spot while his friends chased animals into the snare. The hunters would then quickly grab their clubs and hit the animals on the head, killing them at once.

For larger game, such as deer and bighorn sheep, a hunter used an atlatl, a flat stick about two feet long with notches on one end. Near the middle were two loops for the hunter's fingers. By attaching a spearhead to the notched end, the hunter could throw the spear much farther than he could without the atlatl.

In the backs of some alcoves, the Anasazi dug holes about two feet wide and six feet long and lined them with flat rocks to keep them from caving in. They may have used these holes for storing food, tools, seed, or other items too bulky to carry with them in their travels. Probably the people picked up supplies or restocked the storage holes when they passed by on future hunts.

The rock-lined holes were also used as graves, and in them archaeologists have found the remains of human bodies—many of them infants or small children—from which they have learned much about Anasazi culture. The bodies were wrapped in blankets, arms and legs tucked close to their chests. Beside them were items the dead person might use in future lives, including new sandals, food, tools, baskets, and jewelry. Occasionally the body of a dog, buried with its master, has been found in these alcoves, showing that the Anasazi did keep animals as pets. Thanks to the dry climate of the American Southwest, the bodies have been well preserved, making them easier to study.

BASKETS AND BABIES; CLOTHES AND FASHION

Just as they needed baskets to gather food, the Anasazi also needed baskets for water. To make them, they collected yucca and apocynum, a plant similar to milkweed. Basket Makers twisted bundles of these plant fibers into coils, then wound the coils one layer on top of the other. To hold the layers together they used wide splints, thin but tough strips of woody material. Sometimes they dyed the splints red or black with juices from plants and berries. With the colors, they were able to weave pretty designs into the baskets. To make them leakproof, they smeared pitch—the sticky gum that oozes out of piñon pine trees—over the outside.

The water baskets were tall and cone-shaped so they could be carried easily. For gathering berries, nuts, grasses, and fibers for weaving, the Anasazi made shallow containers that looked like trays. Another style, which served as a plate, was bowl-shaped with a flat bottom. For storing food, the people wove baskets shaped like trunks. There were even pot-type baskets for cooking. These cooking baskets did not go directly into the fire; they only held water. Into the water the Basket Makers would drop rocks heated in the fire. Food would cook in the hot water.

The Anasazi also used weaving when making cradleboards. These resembled small backpacks and were used to carry babies. Cradleboards were made by bending a stick in the shape of an oval for a frame. The frame was covered with a woven crisscross pattern of reeds and sticks and lined with soft juniper bark. For padding, mothers used the soft outer skin of a rabbit's belly, and tied the baby in with a fur cord. There was another use for the soft juniper bark in the Anasazi nursery: diapers.

The Early Basket Makers wove yucca and apocynum fibers into clothing and sandals. Often people had more than one pair of shoes: an everyday pair and a dress-up pair. Sometimes they decorated the dress sandals with buckskin. Whether for dress-up or regular use, sandals were important in protecting the Anasazi's feet from the sharp cactus spines and hot rocks of the dry southwestern land.

The practical, useful design of the sandals was typical of what few pieces of clothing the Anasazi made. From grasses and other fibers they wove apronlike coverings that tied around the waist, the only clothes adults wore during the hot summer months. Children simply went naked. During the winter, the people wore robes and blankets of soft rabbit skin. To be fashionable, women often tied up their hair in buns. Men "bobbed" their hair in three bunches—one on each side of the head and one down the back—tied with a string. To decorate their bodies, they made necklaces and earrings from pretty stones, seeds, and nut shells they found nearby. The Anasazi also used seashells from the Pacific coast, which they acquired by trading with other prehistoric people.

EARLY BASKET MAKER HOUSES AND SETTLEMENTS

As time passed, many Early Basket Makers continued to wander the land, hunting game and gathering food. But gradually they developed a new skill that would completely change their lives: farming.

Since Archaic times, people had known how to grow corn, but the Anasazi now began raising it as a crop for food. At first they raised popcorn, then flint corn, a variety with a very hard kernel. Anasazi women ground the flint corn into meal from which they made corn cakes. To grind it, they put the kernels on a flat stone called a metate and crushed it with a smaller stone, the mano. Some modern native Americans still grind corn this way.

The farming tools of the Early Basket Makers were nothing more than sharp sticks, which they used to dig holes about a foot deep. Into each hole they dropped several corn kernels. As the corn grew, they weeded and hoed with other sharp sticks. They stored part of the harvest for winter use and kept some as seed for the next season.

Raising crops meant that the Basket Makers had to settle down and live in one place. Settling down brought a need for more permanent homes. The first ones, called pit houses, were built over pits or shallow holes in the ground. The pits were dug out in the open, away from the cliffs. Most were ten to twenty

A "mano" or grinding stone, with a lizard figure carved on the surface. *(Courtesy of Mesa Southwest Museum)*

feet across, some larger. The Basket Makers packed the floors with clay and stood poles side by side for walls and roofs, with mud between the poles to hold them together. Not all pit houses had kitchens, for much of the cooking was done outside. The inside of the home was for storage and shelter.

Some of the oldest pit house remains, dating from A.D. 46 to 330, have been found along the Animas River in southwestern Colorado near Durango. Nearby is Mesa Verde National Park. Mesa in Spanish means "table"; verde (pronounced vurd, VUR-dee, or VAIR-day) means "green." Its name tells you that Mesa Verde looks like a green tableland. Although there is no sign here of the Early Basket Makers, Mesa Verde is one of the best-known locations of later Anasazi ruins in America.

The Mesa Verde region was one of three major areas in the Southwest where the early Anasazi settled. They also lived at Chaco Canyon in New Mexico. Today's visitors to the Chaco Culture National Historic Park near Bloomfield, New Mexico, can see 1,800-year-old Anasazi artifacts.

The third area was near today's town of Kayenta in northeastern Arizona. Starting about A.D. 300, the Kayenta people made their homes under cliffs that are located on today's Navajo Indian reservation. Although this area is less well known than Mesa Verde, it has some of the most beautiful and well-kept pre-

ANASAZI TIME LINE			
DATES	PERIODS		EVENTS
A.D. 1- A.D. 500	Basket Maker I Basket Maker II	Early Basket Maker	Nomads live in alcove homes and hunt with atlatls. Slowly they settle down and turn to farming. Craftsmen make baskets but no pottery.
500-700	Basket Maker III	Modified Basket Maker	People build underground pithouse homes. First attempts at pottery making. Bow and arrow introduced.
700-900 900-1050	Pueblo I Pueblo II	Developmental Pueblo	Anasazi move above ground into pueblo-type homes. Many pithouses become kivas.
1050-1300	Pueblo III	Classic Pueblo	Anasazi culture reaches its greatest heights. Multistory pueblos built under the edges of cliffs. More crops grown; finest Anasazi pottery produced. Religious societies formed.
1300-1700	Pueblo IV	Regressive Pueblo	Anasazi leave the northern homelands. Head south and east to mix with other cultures. Time of great change.
1700 - present	Pueblo V	Historic Pueblo	Spanish, Mexican, and American explorers take over ancient Anasazi lands. Pueblo ways of life greatly changed. Some old traditions kept alive.

historic ruins in the United States, many of them built by the later Anasazi.

A NEW WAY OF LIFE

The growth of farming marked the start of a new phase in Anasazi history called the Modified Basket Maker period. The Early Basket Makers modified or changed the way they lived. Basket making was still very important, but more and more people were becoming farmers instead of nomads. This new period would bring with it some of the most important changes in Anasazi history.

Settling Down

On a cushion of grass in Canyon del Muerto—the Canyon of the Dead—two human hands lay in a shallow grave, palms up, still attached to their lower arms. Three necklaces made of abalone shells were strung around the hands. Beside them lay two pairs of sandals, some of the finest ever found. On top of the grave was a basket about two feet in diameter. Many human remains have been unearthed, but none quite so strange as the "burial of the hands."

Canyon del Muerto is one of the most spectacular canyons among the towering pillars of sandstone in Canyon de Chelly. This area is today a national monument in northeast Arizona, but to the Anasazi who once lived here, Canyon del Muerto made an ideal burial ground.

The mysterious hands belonged to an ancient Indian who lived in Canyon de Chelly sometime between A.D. 500 and 700, a time archaeologists call the Modified Basket Maker period. What happened to the rest of the body, no one can say. Perhaps the person was buried by rock falling from one of the high cliffs, and only the arms could be saved for burial.

SECRETS OF THE GRAVE

From this and other graves throughout the Southwest, archaeologists have learned much about Anasazi culture. Modified Basket Makers placed bodies in separate graves rather than burying people together. There were no special cemeteries. Often the graves were beneath garbage dumps. This was not disrespectful; it was the Anasazi way. These practical people had learned that digging was easier in the trash piles than in the hard ground around their homes.

In some of the graves, pipes and parts of games were placed with the dead for use in the afterworld. Jewelry found on the bodies tells us that the Modified Basket Makers had discovered a beautiful gemstone: turquoise. Along with turquoise, Anasazi jewelers often used abalone or olivella shells on necklaces and bracelets. These large, smooth snail shells from the Pacific coast were also traded by the early Indians.

Flutes found in graves tell us that music was part of the Basket Makers' lives. These instruments were made of reeds or hollowed-out bird bones. Some of the flutes still play lovely, clear tones after having been buried for hundreds of years.

This basket was found with other items in an Anasazi grave.
(*Courtesy of Mesa Verde National Park*)

THE ANASAZI POTTERS

Many graves, as well as trash dumps and houses from this period, contained a new item for which the Anasazi would one day be famous: the clay pot. The Early Basket Makers did not know how to make pottery. They had tried molding wet clay into pots and setting them in the sun to dry. But after a little use, they would crack or fall apart. When used to hold water, they simply would turn back into mud. Over time, the potters tried adding grass to the wet clay. This helped to hold the pots together, but they couldn't be used in fires because the dried grass would burn.

18

The Modified Basket Makers were the first true Anasazi potters. Probably they learned the craft from their neighbors to the south, the Mogollon in Arizona. The first step was to find the right kind of clay. There were no potters' wheels in the Southwest 1,500 years ago, so to shape their pots, Anasazi crafters made long ropes of clay. They coiled the ropes around and on top of one another as they did in basket making. The potters then bound the coils together by pinching each new layer of clay to the one below it. To make a smooth surface, they scraped the pinch marks with a piece of wood or broken pottery before firing.

Kilns—special ovens to heat and dry the clay—were still unknown to the Anasazi. Early craftsmen fired their pottery outdoors in very hot fires that quickly burned all the oxygen in the air around them. Pottery fired in this way, without much oxygen, turns gray, and thus gray pottery became the trademark of the Modified Basket Makers. The Hohokam and Mogollon to the south fired their pottery in slow-burning fires that used less oxygen. Because more oxygen was left in the air during firing, their pots turned a tan, yellow, or brown color.

The Anasazi made pottery for practical reasons. They used their jugs and pots to cook and to carry water. But they also liked their dishes to be pretty, just as we do today, so they began adding simple designs. At first they copied their basket patterns, using plant

A piece of pottery from the Modified Basket Maker period.
(Courtesy of Mesa Verde National Park)

juices or powdered minerals to paint lines, circles, and triangles onto the wet clay. Brushes were made of pieces of yucca, chewed until the strands came apart. The stiff, feathery tips were good for painting. When the pots were fired, the painted areas turned black.

Black designs added a nice touch to the pottery. But when the Basket Makers tried to make red pots and jugs, similar to those made by their neighbors to the

south, they didn't have much luck. Pots painted with
red juices or powders simply turned gray upon firing.
The Anasazi didn't understand that it was the oxygen
in the air that made the pots red, not the color of the
paint. Finally in frustration they tried painting the
pottery after they fired it. This worked for a short
time, but soon the paint rubbed off. Apparently the
Basket Makers decided to be content with their gray
pottery, for this is the common color that has been
found.

The size and shape of the fingerprints pressed into
the wet clay when pots were being made once led archaeologists to believe that Anasazi potters were all
women, just as they thought that women cooked
meals and men hunted and tended the crops. But
many experts have since changed their minds, saying
that no proof exists that women made the pottery.

WORK AND PLAY

Pots were not all the Anasazi crafted out of clay. They
also made figurines in human shapes to use in religious ceremonies. Most of the figures were female and
lacked arms or legs. Lines of tiny holes were pressed
into the clay to look like jewelry. Clay figurines, similar to small dolls, have been found in cradleboards,
but there is little other proof that the Anasazi made
toys for their children.

The Basket Makers spent much of their day simply

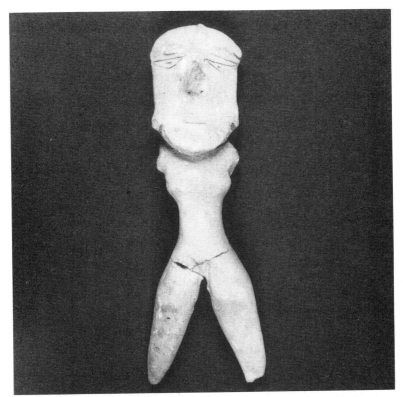

A figurine made by the Hohokam, a prehistoric people who lived in what is now Arizona. *(Courtesy of Mesa Southwest Museum)*

working to stay alive. When hunters returned home with a deer or rabbit, the animals had to be cut, cleaned, and cooked. Hides were tanned to soften them for clothing. Even the needles to sew the hides or the rabbit fur had to be carved by hand from bone. The eyes had to be carefully drilled to avoid breaking the needle.

While the Anasazi spent much of their time working, they still found time to enjoy a few games. Sets of dice have been found among the ancient ruins. Some dice were merely sticks about three inches long, split along one side to make a flat surface. Others were made of bone or clay.

They also played a game whose object was to kick a three- to four-inch wooden ball over an opponent's goal line. Another game involved tossing darts through a small moving hoop made of bent sticks.

BEANS AND CORN: A COOK'S DELIGHT

The Anasazi were adding many new skills to their lives, and their culture was growing fast. Now that they knew how to make pots for cooking, they could put a new food item on their menu. For some time, people had known how to raise reddish-brown-and-white spotted beans. But before the discovery of pots, there was little they could do with them. Beans need to cook slowly for a long time before they are soft and good to eat. This type of cooking just wasn't possible in a basket. With a pot, however, cooks could put the beans in a little water, set the pot in the fire, and go about their other chores while the beans cooked.

Corn was another big item on the Anasazi menu. To make it tasty, cooks ground the hard kernels into various textures of cornmeal with a mano on a metate, just as their ancestors had done. Sometimes they formed the ground meal into balls to be boiled in a souplike mixture; other times they baked it in squares on hot stones. The Anasazi had no sugar for their baking, but they may have sweetened their corn dishes another way—by chewing the cornmeal before cooking. In this way, their saliva turned the starch into sugar, adding a nice flavor to the bread. These prechewed cornmeal balls or cakes were considered a delicacy. The Anasazi also ground dried corn into flour, from which they may have made a tortilla.

A NEW TYPE OF HOUSE

Raising corn and beans brought big changes to the Anasazi way of life. Farmers discovered that beans, in particular, had to be tended very carefully. A field of corn might be planted and left, but beans needed care nearly every day after planting. This encouraged the Anasazi to spend more time at home.

As their homes became more important to them, they began to modify or change the crude pit houses built earlier. They dug deeper pits, some extending down three to five feet, and tried rectangular designs on some. To enter a pit house, a person went through the roof or along a side passage called an antechamber, down into the pit area. Around the inside of the pit were four large posts which held up a platform of logs that served as a roof. Smaller logs sloped from the ground up to this platform, creating walls. Before they learned to make axes to chop trees for the posts, workers burned the trees to fell them.

All pit houses were built in the same basic style. To keep out rain and snow, the Anasazi covered them with a mixture of grass and mud, a sort of adobe plaster. There were no fancy houses for the rich and no shacks for the poor, probably because there were no rich or poor families at this time. The Anasazi seem to have had a fair society where all people were equal.

Some Modified Basket Maker sites had only a few houses; others had as many as a hundred. One mesa-top location in Chaco Culture National Historic Park contains the remains of eighteen houses with a little courtyard in the center. At one time there were forty-eight bins here for storing corn and other grain.

A good place to see the difference between a Modified Basket Maker pit house and those that would be built by the later Anasazi is at Mesa Verde National Park. Here, more than 4,000 ancient ruins are protected by the National Park Service. A pit house built in A.D. 626 stands near the remains of a home built nearly 600 years later. Both are on Wetherill Mesa at Step House ruin, named for the long length of stone steps that the ancient people built as an entryway.

INSIDE AN ANASAZI HOME

Pit houses were much alike on the inside. On the floor were storage pits and bins made of stone. In the center of the roof there was often a smoke hole, for many Anasazi had indoor fire pits. In later years, peo-

These are actually the remains of two pit houses. The one at the top of the photo, built in 674, was destroyed by fire. The second (in the foreground) was built a short time later. In the center, separating the two houses, is a row of sandstone slabs, which was put there to keep the remains of the first pit house from collapsing onto the second. In the foreground pit house, the rectangular hole was a storage pit; the two circles on either side were post holes. The slab of stone sticking up near the middle of the row of sandstone was the deflector, and, just beyond it, the large circular hole is the fire pit. The smallest hole just beyond the fire pit is the *sipapu*. Note the earthen benches around the edge of the pit house; they may have been used for sleeping. *(Courtesy of Mesa Verde National Park)*

ple would enter and leave their homes by a ladder set into this smoke hole rather than through the antechamber.

Building an indoor fire pit that worked well was no simple task. Modern masons who build fireplaces in homes must see that the fire gets just the right amount of air. A fire fed by too little air will die, but one hit by a strong draft also will die. Anasazi builders had the same problems as modern masons. To solve them, they began using the antechambers as air shafts. Between the fire pit and the spot where the antechamber opened into the room, they placed an upright slab of stone called a deflector that kept the draft from blowing right onto the fire and putting it out.

Indoor fire pits made it possible to cook inside. In fact, Anasazi homes had an area that could be called a kitchen. How do we know? Because tools used in food preparation have been found in the same parts of many pit houses. The kitchen and other "rooms" of the pit house were sectioned off by ridges of mud built up from the floor. As years went by, the Anasazi used adobe and built these ridges higher, almost like walls, which made more distinct rooms.

Across the fire pit from the kitchen, many Anasazi families dug a small hole in the floor that the Hopi call a sipapu. It was through a hole just like this, their legends say, that the first people came onto Earth. The sipapu in many Anasazi homes was put there as a symbol to show how people came up from the underworld at birth. Some native Americans in the modern Southwest still dig sipapus in their religious areas today.

A CHANGING SOCIETY

Archaeologists believe the Anasazi were a peaceful people, for no weapons of war have been found among their artifacts. The way they designed their homes is a further clue to their peaceful life. By the beginning of the Modified Basket Maker period, the Anasazi had begun moving into open areas away from the cliffs. They arranged their pit houses in groups. Out here in the open, the people could have been attacked very easily. If they had feared enemies, they would have stayed in the alcoves, under the protection of the cliffs. Pit houses in wide-open areas would be hard to defend.

The 600s brought other changes to the Anasazi, among them a new invention in hunting. Until now, the main weapon of the hunt had been the atlatl. But by the late 600s, the bow and arrow had become part of Anasazi hunting gear. The people probably learned to make this weapon from their southern neighbors, but no one is sure. With bows and arrows, hunters were much better shots than with atlatls. This meant that hunting no longer took as much of their time. They could spend more of their days at home, working on ways to better their lives.

One of the new ideas they tried was taming turkeys. You might think the Anasazi raised these big birds for food, but actually they used the colorful feathers shed by the turkeys to decorate their clothing. Turkey feathers also made warm wraps. Cutting the feathers in half lengthwise, the Basket Makers would wrap them around pieces of rope and tie the ropes together to make feather robes like blankets. Sometimes they added fur for a special touch of warmth in winter. It may have been the children's job to herd the turkeys around like sheep and keep them out of the houses when they got too curious.

The rest of the Anasazi wardrobe looked much like that of the Early Basket Makers. During this period, weavers crafted some of the finest sandals ever made in prehistoric America. The improved sandals had tips that were slightly curved rather than straight across at the toes. Sandal makers built their shoes in two sections. The bottom was a sturdy piece woven in wide strips with deep treads for traction. The top piece was softer and more stylish; weavers used colored cord to make pretty patterns. The improved sandals made walking much more comfortable for the people in this land of thorns and cactus.

THE BEGINNING OF A NEW AGE

The new skills they were learning allowed the Anasazi to do more than simply survive from day to day. Farmers experimented with new crops. Religion became more important, and soon people began building special structures for spiritual ceremonies. By the end of the 700s, the Modified Basket Makers had

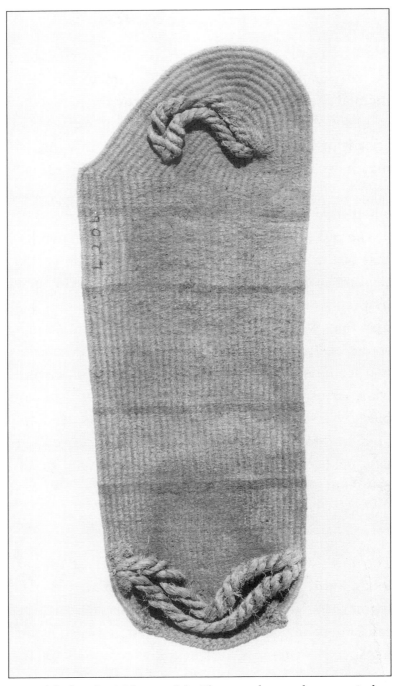

Modified Basket Maker sandals. The curved-toe style was typical of this period. *(Courtesy of Mesa Verde National Park)*

changed their way of life so much that archaeologists began calling them by another name.

Of course, the new skills did not mean an immediate end to all the old ways. Nor did the many changes in the Basket Makers' lives happen all over the Southwest at the same time. Changes came more slowly to some areas than to others. But the date usually believed to mark the end of the Modified Basket Maker period is A.D. 700. A new age was dawning on the Four Corners region.

THREE

People of the Pueblo

The Duplex People, the Condominium People, the Ranch-Style People—is this what historians will call us when they look back to the 1990s a thousand years from now? Will they name us for the kinds of houses we lived in? This is how archaeologists named the Anasazi who lived in the Southwest 1,300 years ago.

The Spanish word *pueblo* means a type of community structure built for many people. Because the Anasazi of this period built these kinds of community houses, archaeologists named them the Pueblo people.

FROM PIT HOUSES TO ROW HOUSES

For some time after the start of the Developmental Pueblo age in A.D. 700, the Anasazi continued to live in pit houses. Near the houses—often on the northwest side—were storage buildings where grain was kept. These granaries looked like pyramids with flat tops. Over time, perhaps because the pit houses were damp and hard to maintain, the Anasazi tired of underground living and began modifying the granaries to use as homes.

Later, as they began building new houses, the people copied the style of the old granary homes. The new houses used poles as a frame. Builders drove the poles into the ground to form a slanting wall and packed an adobe mortar of mud and grass into the cracks. At first these pole-and-mud houses looked much like the granary houses, with walls slanting inward at the top. But gradually builders began placing the poles upright to form straight walls and topped them with flat roofs.

As houses became more rectangular, Anasazi architects made an important discovery. Instead of building separate structures, they could connect them in a row by having two homes share a common wall. Anywhere from six to fourteen single-room houses were hitched together in these rows. Sometimes the row curved, either loosely or as tight as a U. Other times the rows were L-shaped. Some archaeologists think that family groups, or clans, may have lived together within a row of houses. For that reason, these row houses are called clan houses. In the center of the rows of houses there was often a common area or plaza that contained a pit house. This arrangement of clan houses around plazas was the beginning of the Anasazi village or pueblo.

The years from A.D. 700 to 1050 made up the Pueblo I or Developmental Pueblo period. During this time there was a change in building materials as well as design. To the pole-and-mud walls, Anasazi builders now added large pieces of sandstone for strength. Stone replaced poles in wall construction. Roofs were built of long, heavy poles stretched between the walls. Into the spaces between the large poles, builders wedged smaller poles, grasses, and mud.

Anasazi architects used hard stone hammers to chip and chop the sandstone for their walls. When they had carved stones to the proper shapes and sizes, they piled them together in an organized pattern and mortared them with mud. Using stone and masonry made the pueblo dwellings stronger than the earlier pit houses, enough so that people could add a second story to their homes. They built no stairs inside. To enter, one climbed a ladder on the outside of the house and went into a hole through the top. To enter the first-floor rooms, people had to climb down through the rooms on the second story.

KIVAS

Despite the new pueblo-style homes, underground pit houses still served a purpose. Although they were no longer used as homes, the underground rooms often became social or ceremonial centers where people gathered for special occasions. These rooms are called by the modern Hopi word, kiva. The number of kivas in an Anasazi village varied, as the number of churches or community centers varies in a modern city.

Some kivas were simply modified pit houses; others were built from scratch using the pit house design.

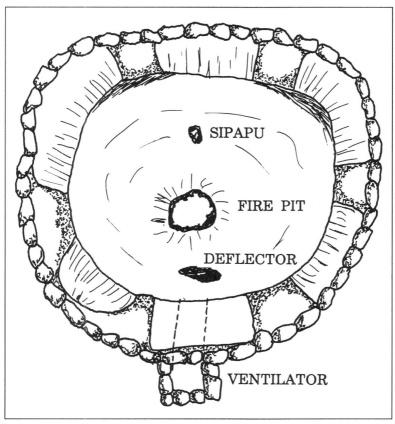

SIPAPU

FIRE PIT

DEFLECTOR

VENTILATOR

A floor plan of a kiva, like the style found at Mesa Verde in Colorado. *(Courtesy of Madison Ayer)*

They were lined with stone, and a stone bench ran along the wall, with pillars rising to support the arched pole-and-mud roof. Kivas also had a sacred sipapu, representing the spot where living things first emerged from Earth Mother. Most kivas had a fire pit in the center, a deflector near the air passage, and a smoke hole in the roof. To enter, people climbed down a ladder through the smoke hole.

For many years, archaeologists thought the kivas were primarily for men. But now some say that women used them as often, particularly during the cold winter months. Because the kivas were underground and had fire pits, they would have been warmer than the aboveground pueblo dwellings.

In winter, when the crops were in, the hunts over, and snow and cold had descended on the Colorado Plateau, people spent long hours in the kivas. Just what kinds of social or religious events took place, we can only imagine. But smoking was probably a part of them, just as it was a part of later native American ceremonies in the eighteenth and nineteenth centuries. A few pipes, some of stone and some of clay, have been found at Anasazi sites. The small number suggests that smoking may not have been common but was reserved for special events.

RELIGION AND NATURE

From what they know about the beliefs and ceremonies of modern native Americans, archaeologists think that religion played a big part in the Pueblo An-asazi's lives. They probably had many gods, each controlling an important power in the universe. The sun god or Father was the most important, along with the spirit Earth Mother. Different gods probably ruled over rain, growth of the crops, the birth of children, and other natural events.

The Anasazi seem to have had a great respect for nature. The medicine man was likely the one who kept the forces of nature in balance. His many duties made him one of the busiest people in the village. Every act of nature had a reason, which the medicine man had to remember and explain to his people. Each village had one or more medicine men who worked with the young men, teaching them their secrets.

The people of the pueblos formed secret societies. Communities might have several societies, each in charge of a different religious or social duty. One would work to ensure good hunts; another to cure illnesses. Still another would ward off witches, who from time to time upset life in an Anasazi village.

One of the secret society's most important jobs was to train Anasazi children in religious matters. Young people reaching the age of twelve to fourteen were ready to be brought into a secret society. To join, they needed a sponsor who helped them learn the ways of the secret society. Often the sponsor was the child's uncle—the mother's brother or another man from the mother's family. Although fathers lived in the same homes with their children, they belonged to different societies than did their wives, and thus the mother's relatives became more important than the father's relatives in the children's religious training.

Training began in the fall, when quiet came over the land. Time spent on hunting and farming could now be freed up for other pursuits. Children studied the myths of their ancestors, along with songs, chants, prayers, and other rituals. They had to pay careful attention during training, for one day they would have to pass along this knowledge to their own nieces or nephews. Training went on around the fire pit in the kiva or in other special rooms in the village. Sometimes the elders would sit for hours with their eyes closed, chanting. During a winter ceremonial, they might stay up all night and spend the next day sleeping. After a child joined a society, he or she often slept in the kiva rather than at home. Married men also went to the kivas when their dwellings became crowded with their own young children or their wives' relatives.

MISSING BODIES AND FLAT HEADS

The Anasazi followed special customs when their people died, one of which is still a mystery. Artifacts indicate that several thousand people once lived in the three major Anasazi centers during the Developmental Pueblo period. Strangely, though, few bodies have been found. What happened to them? Where are the remains of all these people? Why were some buried without their heads and others with only their heads? Why is there no sign of cremation—the burning of the bodies? Possibly some bodies were not buried very deep and were disturbed or unearthed by nature, but this would not account for the thousands of people who must have died.

Many of the remains that have been found were discovered in garbage dumps not far from people's homes. One exception was the children, whose bodies were buried under the floors of their homes near the fire pits. Possibly the mothers placed their children's bodies here so they could continue to look after their little souls. Buried with them were pieces of pottery and other offerings to the gods, among them turkeys and dogs. The turkeys were buried with corn beside them and the dogs with bones.

Another mystery of the grave that has since been solved is the shape of the skulls from this period. The heads of Developmental Pueblo people appeared to be flat and wide—very different from those of the earlier Basket Makers. Archaeologists found so many broad-head skulls that at first they thought they had discovered a new race of people. But further study showed that the "new race" was only the effect of a new style of cradleboard developed for carrying babies. Instead

These boards were used in making babies' cradleboards during Developmental Pueblo times. Note the cord at the bottom that was used to string the boards together. *(Courtesy of Mesa Verde National Park)*

of a padded back for the baby's head, the new models used a flat board. Since a baby's skull is soft, it can be shaped easily. When strapped to cradleboards for many weeks, the babies' soft heads became flat and wide.

Why did the Anasazi want to flatten their children's heads? Maybe it was fashionable. Or maybe they came in contact with people from the east who had flat heads. If these people were more advanced, the Basket Makers may have admired them. In trying to be like them, perhaps they purposely flattened their children's heads.

POTTERS AND WEAVERS

During the Developmental Pueblo time, potters still coiled clay and pinched or corrugated the coils to make their pots. But instead of scraping the pinch marks to form a smooth surface as the earlier Anasazi had done, Pueblo potters left the pinches in place, sometimes even working them into a pattern. Neck-banding was another new pottery style, in which the bowl part of a container was scraped smooth but the neck was left coiled and unpinched. Most neck-banded pottery was a solid gray.

Potters also learned that if they coated their pottery with a glaze of white clay before firing, the surface would better hold a painted design or decoration. At first the designs were small and fine, a combination of dots and thin lines or small geometric shapes. But later craftspeople began using bigger, more solid designs such as triangles and squares.

Weaving remained an important craft of the Anasazi. People still needed baskets and clothing, and the new style of round-toed footwear was becoming popular. Few baskets have survived from the Developmental Pueblo. This is probably not because few were made, but rather because they disappeared or rotted over time.

Among modern Pueblo, men weave the fabrics used in ceremonials. This makes archaeologists think that weaving may have been a man's job in the Anasazi world. To the list of weaving materials, Pueblo craftspeople now added cotton. Anasazi traders had discovered that their neighbors to the south knew how to raise this important crop. But the people of Mesa Verde and Chaco could not successfully grow cotton, for the season was too short, so traders brought back cotton thread, yarn, and cloth to be woven into fabrics.

In time, the southern Anasazi learned to raise cotton. Pueblo weavers built looms to weave the new material into fabrics. In addition to the old fur and feather blankets, they now wove lighter-weight cotton blankets as well. The Pueblo even used cotton for breechcloths, the apronlike pieces of cloth they tied around their waists. To get color into their clothing, they dyed the cotton with natural juices or sometimes painted directly onto the fabric.

VISITING EARLY PUEBLO HOMES

Today, in museums and national parks and monuments, you can see remnants of clothing and sandals worn by the early Pueblo people. You can look at pieces of their pots and tools that they used. At certain sites in the Four Corners region, you can walk by the remains of Anasazi dwellings. Along Ruins Road in Mesa Verde National Park, archaeologists have excavated ruins from the Developmental Pueblo period.

At Twin Trees Village in Mesa Verde, you can see granaries that the pit house dwellers used as storage rooms and later converted to houses. In the ruins of

Horsecollar Ruin, an Anasazi site at Natural Bridges National Monument in Utah. (*Courtesy of National Park Service*)

some Basket Maker pit houses, you can still see fire pits, air shafts, sipapus, benches, dirt walls, and holes where poles were driven to form walls. Twin Trees Village is a good example of how the early Pueblo arranged their homes in rows or units. On the north side of the village is a row of aboveground dwellings and storerooms. In front of the row is an open plaza, and on the far side are the pit houses and kivas.

Another good place to see Developmental Pueblo remains is just south of today's Zuni reservation in west-central New Mexico, an area known as Cibola. Basket Makers first settled this area, but many shards—broken bits of pottery—have been discovered from the early Pueblo. Across the Arizona border they have excavated villages at two locations on the Navajo reservation.

The Developmental Pueblo period was a great turning point in Anasazi history. People's skills in pottery making, farming, and architecture became very developed. But the truly amazing advances were yet to come. The Golden Age of the Anasazi, the period when the Pueblo people advanced to their greatest heights, began in some areas about 1050. During the next 250 years, the Anasazi civilization would reach its peak.

The Golden Age of the Anasazi

On January 22, 1941, a sound like an exploding bomb rocked the dry, treeless Chaco Basin area of northwest New Mexico. The "bomb" turned out to be a giant hunk of stone, named Threatening Rock for the unsteady way it had balanced for centuries. Some people said the rock finally toppled because the gods were angry.

Ancient Indians who once lived here left offerings to the gods behind Threatening Rock. When, in 1940, an archaeologist working in the canyon took those offerings, people presumed the gods got upset and caused the rock to fall. Whether there were any offerings, and whether the archaeologist really took them, is not known. But on that date, Threatening Rock did fall.

THE SHOWCASE CITY

The falling rock killed no one, for the thousand or more Anasazi who once had lived here were long

Pueblo Bonito, one of the largest single Classic Pueblo buildings ever constructed. *(Courtesy of Chaco Culture National Historic Park)*

since dead. But a big chunk of the wall that still surrounded their ghostly city, Pueblo Bonito, was destroyed. For over a thousand years, until the excavations of early archaeologists, the only damage that Pueblo Bonito had suffered was aging from wind and rain, heat and snow. But with the fall of Threatening Rock, thirty of the pueblo's 800 rooms were buried.

The "bomb" came as no surprise to modern-day Navajo. Their ancestors had named the place Sa-bah-ohn-nee, "the house where the rocks are propped up." Threatening Rock did look as if it had been propped up with poles and rocks by the ancient people, perhaps to keep the dirt from eroding and allowing the giant to fall.

Just why the people of Chaco Canyon decided to

build Pueblo Bonito right under Threatening Rock is not certain. But in the rock's shadow, shortly after the year 900, the showcase city of the Pueblo was born. As the population grew, the people added new rooms onto both sides of their original dwelling, extending the chain around in a crescent shape. Over the next 250 years, this structure would become the largest single group of Classic Pueblo dwellings in all of Anasazi country.

Pueblo Bonito was actually a town consisting of one huge building—apartments joined by common walls. At the back, it stood five stories high. Not all of the 800 rooms were built at once; in fact, probably no more than 600 were used at one time. In addition to the rooms, Pueblo Bonito had thirty-seven kivas.

That such a city could be built by hand is remarkable, considering that the Anasazi had no metal tools. Nor did they have animals, like horses or burros, to carry supplies. These ancient people did not even know about the wheel, so they had no carts on which to load big slabs of building stone or timbers brought in from the mountains more than fifty miles away. And yet they built a structure that was home to more than a thousand people and lasted more than a thousand years.

THE PUEBLO AT THEIR PEAK

The period that archaeologists today call the Classic Pueblo began at Chaco Canyon shortly after 900, a little earlier than at the other Anasazi centers. This was the age of large, apartment-like houses, during which the Anasazi reached the peak of their development. They built their best homes using finely cut sandstone and good-quality mortar. They crafted their best pottery, developed excellent methods of farming and irrigation, and generally lived a better life than at any other time in their history.

During this period the three main Anasazi centers—Mesa Verde, Kayenta, and Chaco Canyon—grew larger. People came to the centers from remote towns and smaller pueblos to build apartment-style communities. Of course, not all Anasazi moved into the huge houses; some families still lived in single-unit homes quite far from the main population centers. And not all of the dwellings in the pueblos were huge apartment-style buildings; some homes had only a few rooms for one family group.

Why did so many people decide to come together into community groups? Archaeologists are not sure. Perhaps the structures were built this way for defense, although there is no proof that the Anasazi had enemies. Some buildings had high lookout towers; others had small slits in the stonework, which might have served as spy holes. Walls like the one at Pueblo Bonito surrounded parts of the pueblos, and they had few large doors on the ground level. Probably a pueblo with hundreds of residents would scare off an enemy faster than a handful of small groups scattered over a wide area.

But who was the enemy? Were outsiders moving into Anasazi lands? In times of food shortages, their own people may have been as much of a threat as outsiders. Perhaps the reason for the change in housing had nothing to do with defense. Maybe the people moved into pueblo communities to get away from the wind and cold during harsh winters. There may have been religious or psychological reasons for the change. Or perhaps people simply enjoyed the companionship of a closer community.

NEW HEIGHTS FOR ANASAZI CRAFTS

Whatever the cause, many Classic Pueblo people did move down off the mesa tops and in from the open areas to build their grand apartments under the edges of the cliffs, in the same areas where the Early Basket Makers had once lived. This move brought many changes to the Anasazi way of living.

Until now, each family was responsible for making or growing all the things it needed, from corn to pots. But as the people lived and worked closer together, they began to specialize in one activity. Those who were best at a particular task probably took charge of it for the community. With specialization came advances in crafts: people had more time to spend at one job, so they could be more inventive and improve their skills.

Pottery makers carried their craft to new heights during the Classic Pueblo period. The style most common was black-on-white ware (in talking about pottery, the design color is named first and the background color second). Thus black-on-white ware was a black design painted on a white clay pot. Plant juices and ground-up minerals were used for paint. Designs were usually geometric patterns: diamonds, squares, triangles, bands, trapezoids. Black-on-white ware is typical of Mesa Verde pottery, but the people of Chaco Canyon made similar designs. Farther west, at Kayenta, potters also made black-red-and-white on orange. This is called polychrome ware, meaning "many colors." Sometimes the black design on Kayenta pieces took up so much room that black seemed to be the background color.

Mesa Verde and Chaco potters usually did their painting after the pot was polished, so the design stood out clearly on the piece. They made bowls, mugs, ladles, ollas (water jars), vessels with spouts, canteens, pitchers, bottles—nearly as wide a range of containers as you would find in a modern kitchen. Mesa Verde potters are perhaps best remembered for their mugs. One of the most famous is a double mug from which two people could drink at the same time.

Although pottery was the major craft during Classic

Pueblo times, basket making was still important. Weavers made sandals, baskets for carrying seeds and food, and blankets from cotton and feathers. They also developed a new household item: mats woven from reeds or rushes, used as floor and roof coverings. Many mats must have been made, for many have survived.

The people of Chaco Canyon became skilled jewelers. Along with seashells and stone beads, they used turquoise in their jewelry. They cut, chipped, and pol-

Black-on-red Anasazi bowl from the Classic Pueblo period. (*Courtesy of Mesa Southwest Museum*)

ished this beautiful blue stone and fit it into patterns with other polished rock chips to create magnificent mosaics, necklaces, and pendants. One spectacular specimen from Pueblo Bonito contains 2,500 beads and four pendants, each made of beautifully shaped and polished stones.

THE GOLDEN AGE OF ARCHITECTURE

Pueblo Bonito was not the only showcase city of the Anasazi. Builders at Mesa Verde were at the same time working on Far View, a community that would one day house 400 to 500 people. When it was finished, Far View had buildings at eighteen sites with 375 rooms and 32 kivas, yet it was only one of several communities at Mesa Verde.

The most famous of all the Classic Pueblo ruins at Mesa Verde is Cliff Palace, a dwelling of 217 rooms and 23. kivas, the largest single structure at Mesa Verde. Here, at one time, nearly 250 people lived. F. H. Chapin, one of the earliest modern-day explorers into Mesa Verde, wrote about his first visit to Cliff Palace: "There it was, occupying a great oval space under a grand cliff . . . appearing like an immense ruined castle with dismantled towers."

The purpose of these towers and of others nearby at Hovenweep on today's Colorado-Utah border is still a mystery. Were they lookout towers from which guards could spot enemies? Or were they signaling centers for communicating with distant neighbors? Perhaps they were observatories, used to track the sun, moon, stars, and planets. Possibly they were built to protect an underground spring or other important natural feature. Or they might have been used in Pueblo ceremonials as an extension of the kivas.

Most tower building took place in the last half of the Classic Pueblo period. These towers, like the houses, were of better quality than earlier ones. Early builders had used sandstone blocks that left gaps between the stones when piled on each other. To fill the gaps, masons wedged smaller stone chips into the holes and packed mud mortar in the cracks. On the outside they painted a coating of mud so the stonework was not visible. As the Pueblo learned better ways of cutting their sandstone, their buildings became stronger.

Inside the houses, the rooms were small, not because the people were small but more likely because the rooms were not used much. Folks spent a lot of time outside—hunting, farming on the mesa tops, working in the courtyards in front of the pueblos, sitting on the balconies of their apartment buildings. Darker rooms in the rear were used for storage; front rooms, which were square or rectangular, served as living quarters.

Many of the pueblos had interesting T-shaped doorways. Door openings were two rectangular holes, the top one being a larger rectangle than the bottom, and thereby forming a T. There are many guesses as to why the doors were T-shaped. This design may have cut down on drafts coming into the rooms. Or the shapes may have stood for a particular group or family that lived there. Perhaps the design was for practical reasons: these doorways were easier to enter with a load on one's back. There may have been some religious reason for their shape. No one is sure.

THE GREAT KIVAS

Another interesting twist in building design took place in the kivas. Classic Pueblo people began build-

T-shaped doorways at Spruce Tree House in Mesa Verde National Park. (*Courtesy of Mesa Verde National Park*)

ing storage slots or cubes into the masonry lining of kiva walls. Over the masonry they spread a coat of clay plaster on which they painted murals. The Museum of Northern Arizona in Flagstaff has examples of the kiva murals painted by the later Pueblo people.

Large kivas built for community use were called great kivas. Most were circular and ranged from forty-five to seventy feet across. The great kivas had rooms leading off the main chamber and storage vaults built into the floors. Instead of a circular fire pit in the center, they had masonry fire boxes raised above the floor. Around the floor were masonry benches where people could sit and watch the ceremonies.

Entering a great kiva meant going down a staircase. On the ground level at one end was a platform like an altar. In some kivas an underground tunnel led to this altar. Actors wearing masks and telling the story of the beginning of life may have come out of the tunnel during ceremonies, just as the Anasazi believed that their ancestors had first come to Earth from under the ground. On today's Zuni reservation in New Mexico is a site called Village of the Great Kivas, named for two of the largest kivas yet discovered. The smaller of the two is fifty-one feet across; the larger is seventy-five feet.

DAILY LIFE IN A PUEBLO VILLAGE

The Anasazi's daily schedule depended on the time of year. In winter, the women were probably the first ones up in the morning, rekindling the fires and beginning to prepare the first meal. Children may have huddled around the fire, helping the women fix the food. Perhaps while they waited for breakfast they would drink a cup of thin, hot corn gruel from their mugs. Corn bread and meat, ready about midmorning on a winter day, likely made up a typical breakfast. In late afternoon, the women may have fixed a larger meal of beans or squash, berries, and dried fruits or roots, in addition to corn bread and meat. Although women probably did much of the cooking and child care, they played an equal role with men in the Anasazi society.

During the winter, men and women most likely spent many daytime hours weaving cotton-and-turkey-feather blankets, buckskin robes, and leggings made of human hair. In general, the Anasazi wore loose-fitting clothing like ponchos, which they could tie at the waist for a tighter fit; they made no tailored clothes.

A very important job in the community was gathering water. In winter, finding water was not such a problem, for people could gather snow and melt it over a fire. In the driest months at Mesa Verde, people went out once a day with jugs and came back carrying as much as five gallons of water each—on their heads. The reason they carried the water on their heads was so they could use their hands to climb up the sides of the steep cliffs to the pueblos.

As spring approached and the weather got warmer, the Anasazi were more often outdoors. Just like modern farmers, they began preparing the soil for planting. The cliff dwellers chose the mesa tops to plant their crops, for here was the best sun and a sure target for rain. In areas where the valley floors got plenty of sunshine and rain, crops could be planted closer to the homes.

When heading to the mesa tops to plant, farmers would fill the whole skin of a little deer—feet and all—with seeds. Before they left the pueblo, well-wishers would pour jugs of water over them, which ensured that rain would fall on the crops. Then they would climb to the mesa tops, plant their seed, and pray to the gods for a good harvest. Once the seeds were planted, they had to be guarded against birds and animals day and night. Often children were the guards. As they stood at their posts on dark nights, they might smear ashes on their faces in hopes of keeping away witches who were prowling the mesa tops.

Water was the key to successful farming in this dry plateau country of the Southwest. Without water, the harvest would be poor, and a poor harvest meant illness and starvation in the pueblo. Some groups of Anasazi built fancy irrigation systems to carry water to their crops. In other areas, ditches collected water from rainstorms, and the supply was let out into the fields when necessary to water the crops. Dams along the ditches caught water from heavy summer rainstorms and channeled it into natural ponds or reservoirs.

Another way the Anasazi watered their crops was by terracing. The people of Chaco Canyon and certain other areas built their gardens in stair-step levels so the water would run gradually downhill. In terrace gardening, the water from the upper levels of crops waters the levels below as it flows downhill.

Anasazi engineers built roadways as well as waterways. Their masterpiece was a 400-mile system of roads in the Chaco region. Chaco was a hub, or center, for more than seventy-five towns called outliers.

Anasazi baskets found at Chaco Culture National Historic Park.
(Courtesy of Chaco Culture National Historic Park)

Beginning in the eleventh century, the people built a system of roads to connect these outliers. The longest one ran forty-two miles north from what is today Chaco Culture National Historical Park. The villages along this road were spaced about one day's journey apart. The Chacoan road system was not just a group of travel-worn paths; these were well-planned roads, laid out in straight lines and averaging thirty feet across.

THE GREAT MIGRATION

By now the Anasazi were at the peak of their culture. During the Golden Age, construction, craftwork, and farming all reached new heights. The people combined all the knowledge and skills they had gained over the past thousand years to make their ways of living better, easier, more productive. Then, starting in the mid-1100s, a great movement began. Archaeologists are not sure why, but the Anasazi started moving in from the outlying communities, much as people today might move into the city center from the suburbs.

From Monument Valley in today's northeastern Arizona, people moved south into the canyons of Tsegi, Keet Seel, and Betatakin—the center of the Kayenta Anasazi. At Keet Seel, now on the Navajo reservation, they began building a village. When it was finished in 1286, Keet Seel was home to nearly 150 people. Today it is the best-preserved major cliff dwelling in the American Southwest. Nearby was Betatakin, another Kayenta cliff dwelling, which by 1280 had more than one hundred rooms.

While these dwellings were being built at Kayenta, great migrations were beginning at Mesa Verde and Chaco Canyon. During the Golden Age, nearly 50,000 people had lived in the three major Anasazi culture centers. But by the thirteenth century, beginning at Chaco, they abandoned many of the huge cliff dwellings. Very little home building or remodeling went on there during the Golden Age; the society seems to have stopped growing. Soon, similar migrations would start from other Anasazi communities. For a short time after the Chacoans moved out, Mesa Verde Anasazi seem to have moved in. But by 1300, they, too, were gone.

UNANSWERED QUESTIONS

Drought may have been a major reason for the Anasazi move. Archaeologists can tell, by studying poles cut from trees that grew then, that a dry period came over the Chaco region beginning about 1130. Lack of rainfall likely caused a crop failure, which meant a shortage of food throughout the land. This shortage was probably made greater by the large numbers of people who resettled at the centers.

A great drought also struck Mesa Verde from 1276

to 1299. It did not last as long as the Chaco drought. But twenty-three years is a long time for farmers to grow crops without enough water and for people to live with too little food. Probably they got discouraged, and one by one, families left Mesa Verde.

The Anasazi at Kayenta may have moved into the canyons of Keet Seel, Tsegi, and Betatakin for the same reasons. Kayenta farmers seem to have had problems watering their crops. Perhaps those who moved hoped there would be enough water at the bottoms of the canyons to continue farming. When they found there was not, they abandoned the canyons and were gone by 1300.

The climate may have brought big changes to their way of living. Throughout the world, in the late 1200s, there was a cooling period. This mini–Ice Age probably shortened farmers' growing seasons, causing a shortage of food. This, combined with the drought, could have brought disaster.

Another reason for the great migration may have been increasing danger from outside enemies. Toward the end of the Classic Pueblo period, larger walls were constructed around the pueblos, and kivas were moved inside the walls. Perhaps the enemy were bands of nomadic Shoshoneans who came from the Great Basin region. The raiders could have planned to steal the Anasazi's food supply and rob their fields, which would have meant starvation.

It is possible that arguing and quarreling among the Anasazi themselves was a reason for their leaving. As populations increased and food supplies became shorter, there would have been greater competition for what was available. The Anasazi may have disagreed on how best to handle their situation, and arguing could have led to the breakup of the villages.

Big questions remain in archaeologists' minds. If drought was the reason, why did people living near the rivers, where water was not such a problem, also leave? And if people were suffering from drought, why didn't they move to areas that had plenty of water? In many cases, the Anasazi's new homes were nearly as dry as their old. All that is known for certain is that they did leave.

THE MELTING POT

Throughout history, groups of people have left their villages and moved to new homes. But some of the people, at least, usually stayed in the old homeland. The Anasazi migration was different; all the people left.

They did not, as many believe, simply disappear. They moved to other areas and mixed with the people there to form new cultures. In small groups, the people of Chaco, Mesa Verde, and the San Juan River regions headed south into the land of the Zuni. Some went southeast toward the Rio Grande. Here they mixed with the locals, teaching them their ways and learning from them as well. To the west, the Kayenta and Canyon de Chelly people moved south toward the Hopi mesas and the Little Colorado River. From the mixture of Anasazi and local native peoples came the ancestors of today's Pueblo Indians.

The Golden Age of the Anasazi was coming to a close. After 1300, the people learned no new methods of building, farming, crafts, medicine, or other skills to improve their lives. And, say historians and archaeologists, when a culture stops growing, it dies. Although the Pueblo culture did not die completely, it was no longer pure. Anasazi ways were becoming so mixed with those of their new neighbors that soon the people could no longer be called Anasazi.

FIVE

Goodbye to Old Homelands; Hello to New Neighbors

In the Pueblo religion, the soul of the mountain lion is said to bring hunters success in tracking game. Good luck in hunting was just what the Anasazi of the fourteenth century desperately needed. The great drought had left their farmlands barren, and the growing population had given them more mouths to feed. As they abandoned the centers at Mesa Verde, Kayenta, and Chaco, the Anasazi depended more on hunting game for food.

Part of the huge migration headed south, settling near what is today Bandelier National Monument in New Mexico. Keeping in mind the power of the mountain lion's soul, the people built a shrine to the animal. Today at Bandelier, two lions carved from volcanic rock crouch in a circle of stone. Around them is a row of deer and elk antlers. Modern Pueblo, descendants of the Anasazi, still worship at the Stone Lion shrine.

The Anasazi who arrived at what is now Bandelier were only part of the large group that began leaving their homes in the late 1200s. By 1300, so many Anasazi were on the move, mixing with new neighbors in the lands around them, that their own culture began to change. They were entering a new phase in their history. This period, from 1300 to 1700, is sometimes called the Regressive Pueblo, but this term is not exactly right. *Regress* means to go backward to an earlier way of doing things. Anasazi culture didn't actually go backward; it just didn't go forward. The term Pueblo IV, used by some archaeologists, is probably more correct. Although it's unfair to say that the Anasazi regressed, their way of life did change greatly during Pueblo IV as they traveled into new lands and met new people.

THE ANASAZI IN HOHOKAM LANDS

One of the groups the Anasazi encountered was the Hohokam, who lived in what is now southeastern Arizona. Some of the people on today's Tohono O'odham Indian reservation west of Tucson are thought to be their descendants. Archaeologists do not agree on when the Hohokam culture began, but it is thought to have started about A.D. 1.

The Hohokam and the Anasazi were quite different. Both were farming people, but the Anasazi raised different kinds of corn and beans and used different farming methods than did the Hohokam. They also differed in the way they cared for their dead. The Hohokam cremated their people, but the Anasazi buried theirs.

Hohokam craftspeople produced some pottery, but they were more skilled in stoneware. They carved hoes and other tools of stone, as well as fashioning containers, spear points, and jewelry. Mixing shells with turquoise or other precious stones, they created lovely mosaics. Some rather strange stone items—ear-

Hohokam necklace, made of turquoise and shell. *(Courtesy of Mesa Southwest Museum)*

plugs and nose buttons—also have been found. The ancient people may have attached the buttons through their noses or through the soft parts of their chins to mark their importance in the community. Or they may simply have been following a fashion.

One of the finest structures built by the Hohokam is Casa Grande, "great house" in Spanish. The Casa Grande ruins are now preserved as a national monument south of Phoenix. The great house—the tallest structure in this settlement—stands four stories high and has no windows. People entered through the roof or by small doors on the ground floor. This interesting structure was built from caliche, a type of soil found below the surface of the desert. The caliche was mixed with water to produce a sort of natural concrete. The moist, thick mixture was then packed by hand onto the walls in sections twenty-five inches high. When one section had been patted into place and allowed to dry, the next one was formed. Archaeologists believe Casa Grande was built either as a dwelling or as a ceremonial center, but it was also used as an observatory. Today a roof has been built over the structure to protect it from the weather.

Another Hohokam ruin to survive into modern times was El Pueblo de los Muertos, the City of the Dead, just south of present-day Tempe near Phoenix. This village had thirty-six buildings and many small houses. The largest building was surrounded by a huge wall, seven feet thick in spots. Water for the pueblo came from irrigation ditches dug to the Salt River. Unfortunately, El Pueblo de los Muertos is no longer standing; it was destroyed by modern-day farmers clearing fields for planting.

The Hohokam are best remembered for the excellent irrigation canals they built. Because they lived in one of the driest parts of America, they had to find a good way of getting water from the rivers to their fields or they (and their crops) would die. Canal building was done with the simplest tools: wooden shovels and stone scrapers. The early canals, those built around A.D. 500 or before, were about five feet across and five feet deep. It took thousands of people, working with good plans and good leaders, to build canals in which water would flow freely to the fields. As the Hohokam population grew and the people needed more water, workers dug the canals deeper and wider.

The canals needed constant care, for weeds grew and dirt collected in the bottoms nearly as fast as the people could clean them. But the ditches worked well—so well that in some areas around Phoenix, nineteenth-century American settlers cleaned, repaired, and began using them nearly a thousand years later. Some have been lined with concrete and are still in use.

One interesting idea that may have come to the Hohokam from the Maya of Central America was the building of ball courts. These courts, which can be seen today, were oval and measured up to 200 feet— about two-thirds as long as a modern football field. The game was played by two teams of up to three players each. The object was to hit a ball through rings in the walls of the court without using hands or feet. Players could knock the ball only with their thighs, knees, or backsides. It's doubtful that the game was played solely for fun; probably it was part of a religious ceremony.

When the Anasazi first moved onto Hohokam lands, there was little sharing or exchange of ideas. Each group wanted to keep its own ways and customs. But by the early 1300s, the Anasazi as well as other groups were entering the area in large numbers. What happened when so many people with different backgrounds came together in one place? One group did not take over the other, nor did they fight. For many years the Anasazi and the Hohokam lived side by side in peace. Although they shared ideas, they did not blend completely into one culture; each group kept many of its own traditions.

Hohokam means "those who have vanished." But like the Anasazi, the Hohokam didn't really vanish. After living with people of other cultures for quite some time, their own way of life changed so much that they could no longer be called "true" Hohokam.

THE SALADO AND MOGOLLON

Another group with whom the Anasazi exchanged ideas was the Salado. Their name comes from Rio Salado, Spanish for Salt River, which ran through their homeland near Phoenix. As a group, the Salado did not mix with or move into Anasazi or Hohokam lands. But Salado traders actively exchanged crafts with the locals they encountered. So popular were Salado wares that the Anasazi and Hohokam imitated their styles.

Black-on-white canteen or water jug crafted by the Salado between 1150 and 1350. *(Courtesy of Mesa Southwest Museum)*

Anasazi travelers also met up with the Mogollon, a native group dating back to A.D. 300. The Mogollon lived along what is now the southern section of the Arizona–New Mexico border. Mogollon culture developed more slowly than that of the Anasazi, and just how it developed is one of the great mysteries of southwestern archaeology. Some archaeologists say the Mogollon was simply a variation of the Anasazi and not really a culture of its own.

Like the Anasazi, the Mogollon lived in pit houses, moving to aboveground dwellings about A.D. 1000. They, too, crafted pottery by coiling and scraping, but because of the type of clay they used and the way they fired it, Mogollon pottery was red on brown instead of having a white or grayish background like Anasazi ware.

By 1100, Mogollon ways—among them pottery making—had changed greatly. Through the influence of the Anasazi and other groups, they were now creating a very unique style of black-on-white pottery. Out of these changes, a new culture, the Mimbres, was formed. The unique black-on-white pottery developed by the Mogollon would one day be called Mimbres pottery.

THE NEW CENTERS OF ANASAZI CULTURE

As the people left their old homes and entered new lands, the centers of Pueblo culture changed. No

Casa Grande, or "Great House," stands southeast of today's city of Phoenix. Casa Grande was built by the Hohokam between A.D. 1200 and 1300, and was abandoned by 1450. In 1932 a shelter was built over the structure to protect it from further ruin. (*Courtesy of National Park Service*)

longer were they located at Mesa Verde or Chaco Canyon. A region of flat-topped mountains south and east of the Grand Canyon, and known today as the Hopi mesas, became one of three new centers. Old Oraibi, located atop Third Mesa, is said to be the oldest inhabited town in the United States, possibly settled as early as 1150. When the Anasazi entered this area they mixed with the local people and shared ideas. Descendants of these people and the Anasazi have lived here ever since and are known today as the Hopi.

Like their ancestors, the Hopi became great potters. Between 1400 and 1625 they produced some of the

Hopi children of the late 1800s play in the village of Oraibi, possibly the oldest inhabited town in the United States. Note the ladder leading through the roof into an underground kiva. (*Courtesy of Arizona Historical Society*)

most spectacular pottery ever made. They discovered a new way to fire their pots, using as a fuel the coal that they mined from the nearby mesas. Nowhere else in the New World was coal firing known. Hopi pots were polychrome—many-colored—and had beautiful designs, both geometric shapes and pictures of living figures. Often the background color was yellow, with designs painted in red and black. Today's Hopi women still use the designs of their ancestors to produce lovely pottery.

Many of the homes built during Pueblo IV were made of stone covered with adobe. The pueblos were larger than in earlier years, now covering ten to twelve acres of ground. Plazas separated the long rows of buildings. On the stone-lined floors of the kivas, archaeologists have found parts of looms, showing how advanced the art of weaving had become. Although the modern Hopi do not weave as much of their own cloth as did their ancestors, they do make special clothing and ceremonial blankets. Today, as in ancient times, the men do much of the weaving.

THE RIO GRANDE PUEBLOS

East of the Hopi mesas, in what is now north-central New Mexico, another group of Anasazi—many of them from Mesa Verde—settled in the Rio Grande region through which this big river flows. This was the largest area of Anasazi settlement during Pueblo IV. Here the people were able to keep alive some of their old habits in their new homeland. But as they learned different ways of pottery making, home building, and other crafts, their culture became less and less like the Anasazi of old.

Although many of the newcomers moved into villages, a few groups decided to start new pueblos. One of these, at Bandelier, home of the Stone Lion shrine, was called Tyuonyi, which means "meeting place." Tyuonyi, built about 1420, was a huge circle of dwellings with 300 connected rooms on the ground floor and more rooms behind and above those. In the center was a plaza with three underground kivas on the north side. At any one time over the next hundred years, some 500 people may have lived here. Perhaps to protect themselves from outsiders, the folks at Tyuonyi built only one narrow entrance into the plaza. Across the entrance they drove a row of sharp stakes to further discourage intruders.

Today, descendants of the Anasazi who settled the Rio Grande region still live at Taos, San Ildefonso, Zia, Santa Clara, Cochiti, and other New Mexico pueblos built before and during Pueblo IV. One group settled on the Pajarito Plateau, a mesa formed from volcanic ash and rock that runs along the west side of the Rio Grande. Another group settled what is now the Santa Clara reservation west of Espanola, New Mexico. If you visit the area you can see the Puye ruins, probably built in the late 1300s.

The largest and strongest of the structures built during Pueblo IV was at Pecos in northern New Mexico. This pueblo—east of the Rio Grande where the Pecos River begins—was started before 1300. Descendants of the Anasazi lived here until 1838, and more than a thousand skeletons have been uncovered. Today the ruins are preserved for visitors to see at Pecos National Historical Park, southeast of Santa Fe.

ZUNI: ANOTHER PUEBLO CENTER

The third major Pueblo IV center was the Zuni district, which lay between the Hopi mesas and the Rio

The Pecos Valley pueblo in about 1200, as imagined by artist Roy Andersen. These ruins are today part of Pecos National Monument in northern New Mexico. *(Courtesy of Pecos National Monument)*

Grande, along the Little Colorado and Zuni rivers. The Zuni claim that long ago when the earth was newly formed, their people roamed around and across it, looking for the center. They found the sacred spot in what is today the Zuni homeland of New Mexico.

By the middle of Pueblo IV, there were six settlements near Zuni in a section called Cibola. In each village lived 200 or more people. Their homes were four or five stories tall, and the rooms were connected to each other by small, high doors that were like windows. Since later Zuni women ground corn while men did the weaving, archaeologists imagine that Pueblo IV Zuni lived in much the same way. Perhaps they also dressed in a similar style, wearing dark robes spun from cotton.

The people of Zuni developed a new style of pottery called glazed ware. Glazes were paints with lead added, which left a glossy finish when they dried. The glazes were quite hard to use. Not only might they run during painting, but also they often dried in big globs. For this reason, the potters used glazes only to paint designs and not to cover entire pots. Zuni pottery came in two styles: a dark green on white and a dark purple on white.

The Zuni were also good architects, building some of the finest structures of the entire Pueblo IV period. Using sandstone blocks held together with adobe mortar, they created dwellings like those once built at Chaco Canyon.

Just east of Zuni was the pueblo of Acoma, called "Sky City" because it looked like a fort on top of a high mesa. So high was Acoma that the only way to enter the village was by a steep trail cut into the side of the mountain. A legend says that not far away, on top of Mesa Encantada—the Enchanted Mesa—was another pueblo, also reached by a steep, narrow trail. One day, when all but three women of the pueblo had gone down the mountain to work, a great earthquake struck the area. The three left on top were stranded because the rest could not get back to them, and so they died. Those below had angered the gods, the legend said, which is why they were not allowed back to Mesa Encantada. They went instead to a nearby mesa and became the first settlers of Acoma. Today a hiking path, the Zuni-Acoma Trail, leads people over the rough lava flows of this region, through the ancient Zuni homelands.

Remnants of the once-great Anasazi society were now living in villages spread from the Hopi mesas to the Rio Grande. People of the Rio Grande region were known as the "eastern Pueblo"; those of the Zuni district and the Hopi mesas were the "western Pueblo." With the great migrations finally over, the people began settling down. Each community had its own government, often headed by the religious leaders. They met in the kivas to make rules for governing their villages and tried slowly to rebuild their society. Nearly 400 years had passed, but it looked as if Anasazi culture might finally begin a rebirth.

The Fate of the Ancient Ones

In 1539, a Spanish priest, Fray Marcos de Niza, came north from Mexico with a black explorer named Estéban. They had heard stories of great rich cities in the region and had come to see for themselves.

Estéban and a scouting party went ahead into New Mexico, where he first met the Zuni people. The Zuni refused to believe that a black man would be on a mission for white men. Not only that, they accused Estéban of attacking and murdering women, and so they killed him. Some say the Zuni cut up Estéban's body and sent parts around to each of the villages. Others said they put his body on display to warn future invaders of what might happen to them.

When Fray Marcos heard the news of Estéban's death, he turned back at once, daring to go no farther. From what little he had seen, without ever having entered the villages, he wrote his reports. They told of the great size and wealth of the pueblos and encouraged explorers to return.

Just a year later another group, headed by Francisco Vásquez de Coronado, left Mexico searching for the Seven Cities of Cibola. Those who had been north earlier had reported that the streets were paved with solid gold and that people in Cibola ate from golden plates. When the king in Cibola took his siesta, he was said to lie under a tree full of little golden bells that jingled and put him to sleep.

Coronado and his men had a long, hard voyage. In Zuni, instead of the wealthy cities, they found only a poor Indian pueblo. Here lived a group of simple farmers who had no knowledge of gold or any idea of its value. Disappointed and discouraged, Coronado moved his men to a village on the Rio Grande. Here trouble erupted and some of the local people were killed. Those who were spared fled to a sacred mountain nearby while the soldiers robbed and ruined the ancient pueblo. They found storage buildings stocked with corn, squash, and beans enough to last them the winter. Still hopeful that they would find riches, the Spanish stayed on, but by 1542, Coronado decided the project was hopeless and turned his men back toward Mexico, leaving the Indians to themselves.

THE SPANISH CONQUERORS

Although the next forty years were quiet, this period of peace was about the last between the Pueblo and the Spanish. By 1580, other groups of Spanish explorers were heading north into Pueblo lands. Within eighteen years they had claimed the area for Spain and in 1609 founded the city of Santa Fe.

Because of these intruders, the Anasazi rebirth never happened. This new wave of exploration stopped the progress of the Pueblo Anasazi and nearly doomed their descendants for all time.

Much of the contact between the Pueblo and the Spanish was bad. The two cultures could not get along, and since the Spanish had better weapons, they soon overcame the Pueblo. The Spanish had another advantage: horses. Although the Pueblo had never seen these animals, they realized their value at once. So did some of the fiercer tribes to the east, such as the Comanches and Apaches. These Indians had made a few expeditions into the Southwest, and when they discovered the power of the horse, they returned. They came not only to steal horses from the Spanish but also to steal crops from the Pueblo and make raids on their villages.

The Spanish were tearing apart the native people's way of life, destroying the traditions by which they had lived since the early days. Spanish missionaries tried to make the Pueblo believe in their religion, which many did not want to do. They stole their corn and smashed it down in the fields by riding their horses through it. They beat the Pueblo, hanged some, and made others their slaves. The Spanish intruders brought with them diseases unknown to the Indians, which caused great numbers of them to die.

THE PUEBLO REVOLT

By 1642, the Pueblo had had enough. They raided a Spanish settlement and killed the governor of the Spanish territory. But they were not well organized, and the uprising finally failed. If they were going to stop the Spanish, they needed more people and a good leader. But many of the Pueblo villages were far apart, and the people spoke different languages. It was hard for them to work together as one group.

At last a Pueblo medicine man, Popé, came forward as the leader. He went first to the Taos pueblo in the Rio Grande region. If they hoped to fight off the Spanish, he told the people of Taos, they would have to join forces with other Pueblo villages; they could no longer stay independent. Popé traveled among the other pueblos, even west to the land of the distant Hopi. Each group heard the same thing—they must unite against the Spanish.

The Indians were ready to try Popé's plan, and by 1680 the time had come. Popé sent a messenger among the many pueblos, carrying a rope with several knots tied along it. The knots stood for the number of days that must pass before the revolt was to start.

Through some mix-up, the Spanish found out about the plan. But instead of giving up their idea, the Indians simply started sooner.

They killed nearly 400 Spaniards; the rest fled to safety in the infant city of Santa Fe. There the Indians held them until their food, water, and supplies ran out. When at last the Pueblo allowed the Spanish to leave town, they headed south toward the place where today's city of El Paso, Texas, is located.

This was not the last they would see of the Spanish. Although the Pueblo were able to keep invaders out of their lands for twelve years, there were several raids during that time. Not only did Spanish troops raid the pueblos, other tribes from the north and east continued to invade the pueblos as well. To add to their problems, a severe drought struck the region.

Still, the Pueblo hung on. No other native Americans were as successful in keeping the Spanish out of their lands as long as the Pueblo were. But at last they could hold out no longer. In 1692, Don Diego de Vargas, the Spanish governor of New Mexico, came in with large numbers of men, horses, and weapons. There was no battle; the Pueblo could not fight a force so strong. Besides, de Vargas's men now spread rumors among the different pueblos that caused the natives to distrust each other. Without the strength of the group, the Indians could no longer hold out. In 1692, Pueblo lands became part of Spanish territory.

ADJUSTING TO THE SPANISH

Most of the natives did not resist the Spanish at first. Some Rio Grande Pueblo people fled to Hopi country. Others were curious and wanted to learn more about Spanish ways, so they welcomed the newcomers. Still others were friendly because they thought the Spanish, with their finer weapons and horses, could help them fight off invading tribes from the north and east.

But once the Spaniards began building missions and forcing the Indians to live their way, they became unhappy. The Pueblo people had their own gods, their own religion. They wanted to worship in kivas, not churches. To keep peace, some of them went along with the Spanish and allowed themselves to be baptized. But many never followed the priests' teachings. Most wanted nothing to do with Jesus Christ or Christianity. Still, the priests persisted. They traveled among the pueblos, building churches, baptizing people, and seeing that the Indians celebrated Christian holidays.

In some areas there were revolts. But more often the Pueblo simply gave up, feeling that there was no hope for fighting off the Spanish. The Hopi village of Awatobi was one that gave up. Some years earlier, a mission had been built here by the Spanish, and in 1700 a priest arrived to convert seventy-three Indians to Christianity. When this news spread to the nearby pueblos, the people were outraged. It was autumn, the time of great religious celebration for the Hopi. The idea of having their own people at Awatobi worshiping a white man's god during the holiest of Hopi times was just too much. The Awatobi must be punished, the people of the other pueblos agreed.

All through one late October night, the men of Walpi and the neighboring pueblos prepared themselves. At the first light of day, they gathered on top of Antelope Mesa above Awatobi. Waiting below in the pueblo were the few Awatobi who had said no to the Christians. They would help the group who would soon attack from the mesa top. When the signal was given to charge, one of the helpers below opened the huge wooden door to the pueblo, and in rushed the invaders. There, in a kiva, sat the newly baptized Hopi of Awatobi. Even though they were now Christians, they were making plans to celebrate the special Hopi holy days.

This made no difference to the invaders from the nearby pueblos. They saw no way their people could worship both the Hopi gods and the Christian god. In a fury they heaved a blazing torch into the kiva, setting it afire. Next they ran to other parts of the pueblo, beating and killing anyone who had allowed himself to be baptized or anyone who could not say the traditional Hopi prayers. It took only a few hours. By evening Awatobi was destroyed. Only the few who had not been baptized were allowed to live; they moved to other pueblos. Most of the men of Awatobi lay dead in a village that would never again see life.

Not all the native Americans reacted to the Spanish so violently. Farther south and into Mexico they were more friendly. There, in fact, the Spanish and Indians began almost at once to marry and share each other's ways of life. But in the three centers of Pueblo culture—the Rio Grande Valley, the Zuni-Acoma region, and the Hopi mesas—the natives kept more to themselves. They were trying hard to preserve their culture as best they could.

It wasn't easy. Not only were the Spanish moving in from the south, but also troublesome tribes from the north and east were raiding the Pueblo more and more often. The Ute, the Navajo, and the Apache were

Natives look out across Acoma, or "Sky City," a New Mexico pueblo just east of Zuni, photographed in about 1882. (*Courtesy of Museum of New Mexico*)

among the fiercest and most frequent raiders, particularly after they stole horses from the Spanish.

A TIME OF GREAT CONFLICT

The period beginning about 1700, known as the Modern Pueblo period, was one of great conflict for the Pueblo people. Leaders spent much of their time planning ways to protect their villages from invasion. Even the weather brought trouble. In 1777, a great drought struck the Hopi region. For three years the land was dry and parched. Disease followed drought, and killed off huge numbers of Hopi.

A year before the drought, in 1776, the Spanish priest Silvestre de Escalante had traveled through Hopi country looking for a better route to the Catholic missions in California. While there he had counted the people. There were 7,494. At the end of the drought, a group of Spanish explorers took another count. Only 798 Hopi were left; nearly 9 out of every 10 had died. During this same period, smallpox—a disease brought by the Spanish—hit the Rio Grande pueblos. In just one year, some 5,000 people died. Pecos Pueblo suffered the most, but Zia and San Ildefonso lost more than half their populations as well.

By the dawn of the nineteenth century, Indians from the north were a constant threat to the Pueblos. These people, who were not used to farming or living

An Indian guide leads Father Silvestre de Escalante on his 1776 search for a better route to the California missions. *(Courtesy of Utah State Historical Society)*

in pueblos, preferred to steal from the local people rather than raise their own crops. There was little the Pueblo could do. They had no horses, and their weapons were no better than their enemies'. They couldn't move, for they had nowhere to go. The Spanish had taken over the best land.

TRYING TO PRESERVE THE OLD WAYS

Caught in what seemed to be an impossible situation, the Pueblo stayed and tried to keep the ways of their ancestors. Both the eastern and western groups continued to farm. Along the river bottoms in the Rio

Modern Native Americans preserve the old way of grinding corn with a mano and metate. *(Courtesy of Jeanne Broome)*

Grande region, the people raised corn and cotton. In the west, where water was not so plentiful, they tried irrigation. Many crops failed, but still the people farmed. Women and children helped stock the kitchen by gathering berries, herbs, and nuts. In the eastern villages, where the men were often away hunting, women tended the crops.

The eastern mountain pueblos of the Rio Grande had hunting societies. Deer and antelope were the main targets of the hunt. But the far eastern villages, such as Taos and Picuris, sometimes sent hunting parties onto the Great Plains in search of bison. Nearly all the pueblos held rabbit hunts, and even the smallest children took part.

In winter the hunting societies at Taos and other pueblos put on grand and mysterious dances. Dancers wore costumes made of deer or bison skin—heads and all—to make themselves look exactly like the animals they hunted. Other dancers played the role of hunters. They dressed in fancy masks, painted their bodies, and carried hunting weapons. A chorus, sometimes made up of hundreds of people, would sing and chant. Often the dances lasted all day and into the night. And if the gods were pleased, they would see that the hunt was good.

In the west, where hunting was less important, there were secret social societies. Just what went on at these gatherings was known only to the people of that pueblo, and sometimes to only a few of them. There were special ceremonies to bring rain, to ensure the safety of the pueblo, to bless a child who was about to become a man or woman, and for many other reasons.

The Hopi and Zuni pueblos used kachinas in their secret societies and in fact still use them today. Kachinas were spirits that acted as middlemen between the gods and the people. They carried messages to the gods who ruled hunting, harvests, and other important events. Kachinas were the spirits of animals, birds, insects, plants, people—even places—and each had a particular purpose.

The word *kachina* had three different meanings. It

was used to talk about the spirit that it represented. These spirits were said to live half of the year in the San Francisco Peaks north of present-day Flagstaff, Arizona. The other half, until the end of July, they spent in the pueblos with the people.

Kachina could also refer to the men who dressed up as spirits and performed dances while the kachina spirit was in the pueblo. These dancers wore special kachina masks decorated with horns and feathers. Although the mask made him look like the spirit, the dancer himself did not change. He did not become the spirit, but the spirit was thought to live within his soul. If the dancer did a good job, the spirit would allow itself to be seen by the people of the pueblo.

Kachina was also the word for the dolls the Pueblo used to teach their children about the kachina spirits. These dolls were carved and decorated to look like each of the spirits. Since there were more than 250 different kachina spirits, it took the children many hours of study to learn about them. Thirty of the kachinas were more important than the rest. These were the spirits who had contact with the most powerful gods, the ones who controlled the very important things of life.

It was to these gods that the Pueblo of the early 1800s began to pray more and more often. No longer did they pray just for rain or good crops. They prayed now for protection from the white man's diseases and

Hopi Kachina doll, used to teach children about Kachina spirits.
(Courtesy of Jeanne Broome)

for the strength to resist their enemies. The Pueblo population was dropping rapidly. When the Spanish first arrived, they found sixty-six different villages; by 1800, only nineteen remained.

THE END OF SPANISH RULE

In 1810, an event began that at last would help the Pueblo. For some time, Spain had been losing control over Mexico and its other lands in the Southwest. Not only did the Mexicans want to be free from Spain but they also wanted to control the lands to the north, and they were ready to fight. On September 16, 1810—today celebrated as Mexican Independence Day—the Mexicans declared war on the Spanish. For eleven years, fighting raged. When it was over, Mexico was not only free but also ruled the land of the Pueblo and many other parts of the Southwest as well.

The Mexicans soon learned that their new lands to the north were being raided by Navajo and Apache warriors. So bad did the raids become that the Mexicans joined with the Pueblo to fight together against the invaders. Each side fought bitterly. When they could, the Mexicans captured Navajo or Apache children and raised them as slaves. This constant fighting might have gone on longer had not another major change taken place.

Hundreds of American explorers and trappers were now heading west. Their stories about the new lands lit a fire in the hearts of many easterners. Soon, more and more Americans joined the westward movement, and the Mexicans were upset. Their new lands in the west were being overtaken by Anglos. In 1846 a war broke out between the United States and Mexico. At its end, two years later, Mexico had lost control of all the land that is today's American Southwest. The Americans had taken over.

AMERICA MOVES IN

The American victory was good news and bad news for the Pueblo. The good news was that the Americans had the strength needed to fight the raiding Navajo and Apache. The government gave the Pueblo guns and horses to help them fight, but there was one rule. They were not to raid Navajo or Apache camps; they were only to protect themselves. The plan seemed to work; by the 1870s peace had come at last to the Pueblo villages.

The bad news was that with the Navajo and Apache gone, more Mexicans and Americans started moving onto Pueblo lands. Until now, Indian country had seemed too harsh for them. But without the threat of raids, it began to look like a good place to raise cattle and sheep, which need lots of grazing land. Some of this land the ranchers bought, some they got through a plan set up by the government, and some they simply stole or took over. The Pueblo had no papers saying the land was theirs.

The settlers took over the land, but they harmed it. Into the eastern pueblos they brought too many sheep and cattle to graze. The large numbers of animals soon stripped the land of grasses and plants. Americans from the wetter, greener states back east didn't seem to realize that the dry western land was more delicate. Without plant roots to hold the soil in place, there were floods when it rained; erosion washed away much of the land. For the Pueblo people, this meant that food became scarce once again.

Food was scarce in the Hopi country to the west for another reason. Just as peace with the Navajo and Apache finally came, a drought struck. The Hopi had always kept three years' supply of food on hand for emergencies. But even this supply was used up before the drought ended. In desperation, they went to the new capital of Arizona Territory and begged the white men for help. Because they could not understand them, the white men threw the Hopi in jail. Upon their release, they were told that the government had no way to help them.

As in the past, disease followed drought; large numbers of Hopi died from smallpox. Many who were left moved east to Zuni lands. The Zuni welcomed them and taught them many of their ways—pottery design, dances and ceremonials, silversmithing, even a little of the Spanish language.

HANGING ON

Seeing that it was time to solve the problem of who owned Indian lands, the U.S. government made deals called treaties that were supposed to be fair trades of land for money or goods. But seldom were they fair, and often they were broken. The government set aside sections of land called reservations for certain Indians. The tribe as a whole, not each person, would own the land. Reservations had been set up in other parts of the United States, but so far the government had done nothing to protect Pueblo land. Finally, in 1882, the Hopi reservation was established near Black Mesa, their ancient homeland. One group of Pueblo now had some land it could call its own.

But the Hopi soon discovered problems with reservation life. For one thing, their children had to go to the white man's schools. The government set up a school at Keams Canyon, where the children were sent to live as well as study. Many of the Hopi did send their children, but the people of Oraibi and certain other pueblos refused. The government even started an Indian school far away in Pennsylvania. Leaders hoped that when Pueblo children were separated from their parents and villages, they would quickly pick up the white man's ways. By 1889, ninety-two

Pueblo children had gone to the Pennsylvania school. Although many people did not want to send their children away into the unknown world of the white man, most did follow the rule. By the early 1900s, nine out of every ten Pueblo children were attending a white man's school.

The Pueblo had other reasons to be upset with the white man. When Americans first appeared in Hopi villages, the Indians had let them watch their sacred ceremonies. One missionary learned the Hopi language and watched the religious rituals carefully during the ten years he lived in Hopi country. When he returned to the East, he wrote a report telling all about the ceremonies. The Hopi were very upset and kept their religion a secret after this. Other Americans brought back carvings, masks, pipes, and other sacred objects from Pueblo country. They put these on display at the 1893 World's Columbian Exposition in Chicago, which upset the Hopi even more.

Both the eastern and western Pueblo now kept more and more to themselves. What they wanted most was to save what was left of their culture and their people. By the late 1800s, with their population down to 9,000, peace at last began to settle over Indian country. Slowly the Pueblo increased their numbers. By the mid-1950s, there were twice as many Hopi as there had been a century earlier; about 5,000 lived on the Hopi reservation in Arizona. In the eastern villages of New Mexico, some 25,000 Indians were scattered among the eighteen pueblos.

This was all that remained of the once-great Anasazi culture. If the ways of the basket makers, the potters, the weavers, and the medicine men of the kivas were going to survive, it would be up to these modern Pueblo to carry them on.

The Anasazi in Our Time

It was a cold, snowy day in the year 1888. Along the top of a mesa in southwestern Colorado, two cowboys, Richard Wetherill and Charles Mason, were herding cattle. As they looked out across the broad canyon before them, they saw a land camouflaged in winter—a jigsaw puzzle of whites, browns, and grays. Douglas fir trees supplied touches of green. Such a hidden picture maze it was that Wetherill and Mason had a hard time believing what they saw. Across the rocks and treetops, tucked under the edge of a long cliff, was what seemed to be a group of sandstone houses, some of them several stories tall. Wetherill and Mason had ridden horses here for years and never seen a sign of any people. Who, then, lived in these houses? They decided to ride down for a closer look.

What Charles Mason and Richard Wetherill discovered was Cliff Palace, in what is now Mesa Verde National Park. Although other white men had passed

Spruce Tree House at Mesa Verde National Park in Colorado. Underneath the flat area in front is a trash dump. Often the Anasazi dumped trash behind their living areas as well, way back under the alcoves. The uncovered pits are kivas; the ladders visible in the square holes also led down into kivas. Notice that many of the structures have more than one story. The rooms—each one about 6 × 8 × 5½ feet—were used as bedrooms or work areas. *(Courtesy of Mesa Verde National Park)*

through the area before them, they were the first to tell the world what they had found. Here, waiting for nineteenth-century archaeologists to excavate them, were the Anasazi ruins abandoned some 600 years earlier. Not since the late 1200s had anyone lived at Mesa Verde. Pressing on in excitement, the cowboys rode next into the ruins of Spruce Tree House. Here they found more of the same grand houses long ago abandoned. These quiet, ghostly ruins were all that remained of the once-thriving villages at Mesa Verde.

SURVIVING INTO THE PRESENT

Ancient ruins are not the only reminders of the Anasazi in today's American Southwest. Their descendants still live in the Hopi, Zuni, and Rio Grande regions of Arizona and New Mexico. Pueblos like Taos and San Ildefonso, along with the Hopi and Zuni reservations, are centers of modern Pueblo life.

Of course, daily life is not just as it was in Anasazi times. Many modern Pueblo live in reservation houses with electricity and television sets. Others have homes built of dried mud and stone like their ancestors used. Barefoot children run in the dirt roads around the pueblos as they did in ancient times, but in many villages they must now watch for cars. Parts of modern Pueblo festivals and rituals have been passed down from grandparent to grandchild since the days of the Anasazi. But over the years, many of the chants, songs, and dances have been forgotten, replaced by more modern music. Today's Pueblo children have American names and speak English. Many of them do not speak the language of their ancestors.

Even though the modern Pueblo do not live as their ancestors did, they have kept alive many of the ancient crafts. Descendants of the Anasazi are some of the finest craftspeople in the world. Selling their work

Mugs from Mug House at Mesa Verde National Park. Charles Mason, one of Mesa Verde's earlier white explorers, said, "Of all the houses the one most remarkable for what we found in it was the Mug House, so named because of four or five mugs found tied together with strings through their handles." *(Courtesy of Mesa Verde National Park)*

is a major way of making money for the Pueblo. Using their talents to make money began back in the mid-1900s when the government saw what a demand there was for Indian crafts. Leaders tried to help the

Taos Pueblo near Taos, New Mexico. For nearly 1,000 years, Native Americans have lived at or near this pueblo. Today, Taos is the largest multistoried pueblo still standing in the United States. You can visit Taos Pueblo and watch some of the native ceremonies, such as the Turtle Dance in January, corn dances during the summer, and the Deer Dance on Christmas Day. *(Courtesy of Don Laine)*

native Americans build their businesses by setting standards for their work. Only pieces of the highest quality, made by true native people, could carry the government seal. Buyers from the East looked for this seal to assure them that the craft was not just a cheap imitation. Over the years, modern Pueblo craftspeople have brought back basket making, pottery, and weaving and learned the art of silversmithing.

FETISHES AND KACHINAS

One of the most interesting of these ancient arts is the making of fetishes by the Zuni people. Since the early days, figurines or carved figures had been part of their ceremonies. A Zuni legend tells of the time when the gods turned all the animals to stone, and from this story, the idea of making fetishes began. A fetish is a small object made of stone, shell, antler, bone, or other material, in which a spirit is said to live. These spirits are supposed to help people in hard times by doing things like healing the sick, scaring off witches, and ensuring a good hunt or harvest. Fetishes are treated very carefully and specially; when not in use they are kept in a fetish jar and "fed" cornmeal or pollen.

Today's Zuni are masters of fetish carving. Many of their fetishes are animals, some of which stand for directions. The mountain lion fetish stands for north—remember the lions at Bandelier? A wild cat represents the south, east is the wolf, and west is the bear or coyote. While most Americans use only four directions, the Zuni add two more. Zenith, represented by the eagle fetish, is directly overhead. Nadir, the mole, is straight down into the ground.

The Zunis also carve kachina dolls, but the Hopi are much better known for this craft. Kachina dolls do not date back to early Anasazi times. Although they have been in use since before 1600, few were made until after the mid-1800s. The dolls, which can be small and simple or large and fancy, are still used to teach children about the kachina spirits. They are not meant to be spirits themselves. Men carve the figures from the roots of cottonwood trees, cover them with a white clay, and then paint and decorate them to look like the spirits they represent. Kachina dolls are treasured items today; collectors buy and sell them for large sums of money.

MODERN WEAVERS

The oldest of the Anasazi crafts to survive into the modern world is basket making. Unfortunately for today's basket makers, people are not willing to pay as much for baskets as they are for other craft items. Willow and yucca, two of the plants most needed for

Modern-day basket maker Barbara Juan carries on the ancient Anasazi craft of basket making. *(Courtesy of Jeanne Broome)*

weaving, have nearly disappeared in some areas, forcing basket makers to travel long distances to find supplies.

The Hopi are perhaps the best-known of the Pueblo basket makers. People in the Rio Grande pueblos use baskets, but they do not make their own. Instead, they trade for or buy them from other tribes. Many Hopi baskets are not made to be sold, but rather to be given away at weddings and other events. These baskets are woven of wicker, a thin twig dyed in bright oranges, reds, yellows, violets, and even shades of turquoise. Baskets made for everyday use are often less colorful. Kachina figures are a popular design woven into the baskets. Weavers also use animal, plant, and geometric patterns.

Weaving is only one way of making baskets. Another is coiling—twisting plant fibers into coils, with one coil wrapped on top of another, as the ancient Basket Makers did. Coil baskets come in all sizes and shapes, some wide and shallow, others deep and rounded. The coil method is also used to make plaques. These flat, woven circles with pretty designs are given as gifts and awards, or used as wall decorations.

Weaving blankets and rugs from wool and cotton is another craft that dates back to Anasazi times. As in the past, today's weavers are often men. Mats, blankets, and other creations are made of plain earth-tone colors—white, tan, brown, black. Designs are simple stripes or zigzags.

After the uprising against the Spanish in 1680, many Pueblo from the Rio Grande valley fled west into Navajo country. They taught their new neighbors the craft for which the Navajo would one day be famous: the weaving of rugs and blankets. Once they learned the skill, the Navajo developed their own style, using dyes to make different shades of wool and designing more complex patterns. Although the Pueblo were the ones who taught weaving to the Navajo, today's Hopi are the only Pueblo who still do much weaving. Most of the rugs and blankets produced for sale in the Southwest are made by the Navajo of Arizona and New Mexico. Collectors pay high prices for Navajo weaving.

WORKING IN SILVER AND CLAY

The Pueblo taught weaving to the Navajo, but the Navajo, in turn, taught the Pueblo to work in silver. Thanks to the Navajo, today's Pueblo Indians make beautiful silver jewelry. About the mid-1800s, Mexican traders began coming to Navajo lands, offering the natives silver trinkets. The Navajo learned silversmithing and became very good at it. They, in turn, taught the Zuni who, with the help of American traders, learned to cut turquoise and other gems and set them in the silver. The Zuni then shared their new skills with the Hopi. Today the Hopi and Zuni produce some of the most striking silver jewelry in the world.

The craft for which the Anasazi were best known—pottery making—is the one for which their descendants are also best known. Potters from the Rio Grande pueblos of Santa Clara and San Ildefonso are the most famous, among them Maria Poveka Martinez from San Ildefonso. Her pottery has been shown in museums and collections around the world. The style that Maria made famous is a polished black ware decorated with matte (unpolished) black designs.

Maria signed her name to her work, as do many modern Pueblo potters. But in the days of the Anasazi, there was no need to sign. For one thing, the pieces were made for everyday use and were not meant to be sold. Also, every potter knew every other potter's style; there was no reason to put one's name on a piece.

Today the potters of one area, while they may try many styles, usually become known for one particular kind of pottery. In the Santa Clara and San Ildefonso pueblos, the special pottery is a highly polished black or red ware, with animal or geometric designs. Pottery from the western pueblos of Acoma and Laguna has a white or light tan background. Plants, flowers, and geometric shapes are painted in gray, brown, and

Maria, the potter of San Ildefonso, uses a polishing stone to put the final touches on one of her beautiful pots. This photo was taken in about 1937. *(Courtesy of Museum of New Mexico)*

tan. Acoma ware is the lightest in weight and the thinnest of all modern Pueblo pottery. Farther west, in Hopi country, most of the clay is crafted by the people of First Mesa. Much of it is a rich yellow-orange or light brown, some plain and some with designs. The Pueblo Museum in Albuquerque has examples of the styles of crafts found in each pueblo.

Modern Pueblo potters use many of the same methods as their Anasazi ancestors. They start with local clay and mix it with sand or grit to give it strength through the firing process. The clay mixture is rolled into coils, then stacked and formed into the basic shape of the pot or bowl. Next comes the finer shaping and molding, after which the piece is scraped and smoothed with a slice of gourd. The Pueblo, like the Anasazi, never use a potter's wheel to shape their pieces. Before firing, a fine mixture of clay and water called slip is painted over the piece to make a smooth surface. Then it is polished with a smooth stone.

Using yucca leaves as a paintbrush, potters create their designs with dyes or paints made from natural sources: plants, animals, or minerals. Next the pieces are put on a metal grate and fired in a simple kiln for about two hours. The fuel is animal manure packed around the pottery, which keeps the kiln at a temperature of about 1,300°F.

These methods of pottery making have been handed down from one generation to the next, from the Anasazi to the modern-day Pueblo. Maria Martinez, the potter of San Ildefonso, learned the craft from her aunt when she was seven or eight years old. But Maria had no daughters to teach, only sons. "I wish I had a girl," she sometimes said, "so I teach the pottery. [But] I'm happy. And I say, the Mother Earth will help, and then teach their children that are coming." For a time, Maria taught at a government school in Santa Fe. She worked with "the younger people from different pueblos. And now those ladies have . . . children, grandchildren, married. But some still come and visit me and thank me for what they learned from me. So I said, God gave me that hand, but not for myself, for all my people."

Visiting the Anasazi Today

You can visit the pueblos and reservations where descendants of the Anasazi live today. At places like Taos Pueblo in northern New Mexico, the Acoma and Zuni reservations in western New Mexico, or the Hopi reservation in northern Arizona, you can watch native artists making beautiful craftwork using methods handed down to them from their early ancestors.

There are also many national parks, monuments, and heritage centers in the southwestern United States where you can see Anasazi ruins and artifacts. These places have been set aside as special spots to visit for two reasons. The first is to help us learn more about how the Anasazi and other prehistoric people lived. The second is to protect these ruins so that future visitors will be able to see them as well.

When we visit the Southwest and explore for ourselves, we must remember to be respectful and careful of the ruins and artifacts. Many people are not. At one southwestern site, in just one recent year alone, more ruins and artifacts were destroyed by careless visitors than have disappeared naturally since the ruins were abandoned some 700 years ago. We are now the keepers of the Anasazi ruins. What we have is all there will ever be; there are no more ancient people to rebuild what we break. It is up to us to respect these ruins, learn from them, and keep them safe for those who will come after us.

PLACES TO VISIT

ARIZONA
Canyon de Chelly National Monument, Chinle; Navajo National Monument, Tonalea; Glen Canyon National Recreation Area, Page; Grand Canyon National Park, Grand Canyon; Casa Grande Ruins National Monument, Coolidge.

COLORADO
Anasazi Heritage Center, Dolores; Mesa Verde National Park, Mesa Verde NP; Hovenweep National Monument, Cortez.

NEW MEXICO
El Morro National Monument, Ramah; Pecos National Historical Park, Pecos; Bandelier National Monument, Los Alamos; Chaco Culture National Historic Park,

Bloomfield; Aztec Ruins National Monument, Aztec; Salinas Pueblo Missions, Mountainair.

UTAH

Canyonlands National Park, Moab; Natural Bridges National Monument, Blanding.

FOR FURTHER READING

Ambler, J. Richard. *The Anasazi*. Flagstaff, AZ: Museum of Northern Arizona Press, 1989.

Amsden, Charles Avery. *Prehistoric Southwesterners: From Basketmaker to Pueblo*. Los Angeles: Los Angeles Southwest Museum, 1949.

Ayer, Eleanor H. *Indians of Colorado*. Frederick, CO: Jende-Hagan Bookcorp, 1981.

————. *Hispanic Colorado*. Frederick, CO: Jende-Hagan Bookcorp, 1982.

————. *The Anasazi: A Guide to Ancient Southwest Indians*. Frederick, CO: Renaissance House Publishers, 1991.

Bahti, Tom. *Southwestern Indian Arts and Crafts*. Las Vegas, NV: KC Publications, 1966.

————. *Southwestern Indian Tribes*. Las Vegas, NV: KC Publications, 1968.

Brain, Jeffrey P.; Copeland, Peter; de la Haba, Louis; Harrell, Mary Ann; Loftin, Tee; Luvaas, Jay; and Schwartz, Douglas W. *Clues to America's Past*. Washington, DC: National Geographic Society, 1976.

Branigan, Keith. *History as Evidence: Prehistory*. New York: Warwick Press, 1984.

Coe, Michael, Snow, Dean, and Benson, Elizabeth. *Atlas of Ancient America*. New York: Facts on File, 1986.

Dale, Edward Everett. *The Indians of the Southwest*. Norman, OK: University of Oklahoma Press, 1949.

Ferguson, William M. and Rohn, Arthur H. *Ruins of the Southwest in Color*. Albuquerque: University of New Mexico Press, 1987.

Grant, Campbell. *Rock Art of the American Indian*. Golden, CO: Outbooks, 1967.

Jones, Dewitt and Cordell, Linda S. *Anasazi World*. Portland, OR: Graphic Arts Center Publishing Co., 1985.

Lister, Robert H. and Lister, Florence C. *Mesa Verde National Park: Preserving the Past*. Mancos, CO: ARA Mesa Verde, 1987.

————. *Chaco Canyon: Archaeology and Archaeologists*. Albuquerque: University of New Mexico Press, 1981.

Manley, Ray. *Ray Manley's Southwestern Indian Arts & Crafts*. Tucson: Ray Manley Photography, 1975.

Oppelt, Norman T. *Guide to Prehistoric Ruins of the Southwest*. Boulder, CO: Pruett, 1981.

Pike, Donald G. *Anasazi: Ancient People of the Rock*. New York: Crown, 1974.

Robbins, Maurice (with Mary B. Irving). *The Amateur Archaeologist's Handbook*. New York: Harper & Row, 1981.

Rollin, Sue. *The Illustrated Atlas of Archeology*. New York: Warwick Press, 1982.

Scully, Vincent. *Pueblo: Mountain, Village, Dance*. New York: The Viking Press, 1972.

Silverberg, Robert. *The Old Ones: Indians of the American Southwest*. New York: New York Graphic Society, 1965.

Spicer, Edward H. *Cycles of Conquest*. Tucson: University of Arizona Press, 1962.

Spivey, Richard L. *Maria*. Flagstaff, AZ: Northland Press, 1979.

Tamarin, Alfred and Glubok, Shirley. *Ancient Indians of the Southwest*. Garden City, NY: Doubleday, 1975.

Underhill, Ruth M. *First Penthouse Dwellers of America.* Santa Fe, NM: William Gannon, 1976.

Watson, Don. *Indians of the Mesa Verde.* Mesa Verde National Park, CO: Mesa Verde Museum Association, 1961.

Wormington, H. M. *Prehistoric Indians of the Southwest.* Denver: Denver Museum of Natural History, 1947.

Zwinger, Ann. *Wind in the Rock.* New York: Harper & Row, 1978.

INDEX